DATE DUE

DEMCO 38-296

PLANNING LIBRARY FACILITIES:

a selected, annotated bibliography

by
MARY SUE STEPHENSON

The Scarecrow Press, Inc.
Metuchen, N.J., & London
1990

British Library Cataloguing-in-Publication data available

Library of Congress Cataloging-in-Publication Data

Stephenson, Mary Sue.
    Planning library facilities : a selected, annotated
bibliography / by Mary Sue Stephenson.
        p.   cm.
    ISBN 0-8108-2285-7 (alk. paper)
    1. Library planning--Bibliography. 2. Library build-
ings--Bibliography. 3. Library architecture--Bibliog-
raphy. I. Title.
Z679.5.S73   1990
016.022'3--dc20   89-70043

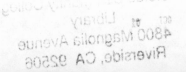

TABLE OF CONTENTS

INTRODUCTION

At some point during their careers most librarians participate in the planning and implementation of a new library facility or the renovation of an existing one. While several library education programs offer courses in facility planning, most currently practicing librarians have not taken such a course. As a result librarians confronted with such a facilities-related problem typically find themselves decidedly unprepared to successfully organize or participate in such a project. A common response to this predicament is for the librarian to turn to the literature for guidance and information. Unfortunately such a move often results in a great expenditure of time with relatively unsatisfactory results, since it rapidly becomes apparent that accessing the library facility design literature is not a simple process.

When they first approach the standard secondary sources librarians and students find an apparently substantial body of literature, but one that is quite difficult and frustrating to master. Items are indexed under a large number of headings and these headings maintain little consistency between the different indexing and abstracting sources. Many relevant materials originate outside librarianship and are not easily identified without checking a number of sources. This selected and annotated *Bibliography* gathers together for the first time a substantial portion of this literature. It has been prepared to assist practitioners, administrators, library educators and library school students.

SCOPE

A pool of over 1400 items was identified during an initial literature review. Numerous secondary sources were checked, using both manual and computer-based strategies, including *Library Literature, Library and Information Science Abstracts, ERIC, Information Science Abstracts, Dissertation Abstracts, Books in Print, NTIS, LC MARC, Psychological Abstracts, Sociological Abstracts, The Architecture Database* and *Conference Papers Index.* Additional items were noted for possible inclusion by checking the bibliographies of identified items. Most of these 1400 documents were examined and a final set of 800 was selected for inclusion in the *Bibliography.* The following criteria were used to determine which items were included:

* Materials concerned with the planning, design and evaluation of library buildings and facilities.
* Materials published from 1970 to mid-1988.
* English language materials, with an emphasis on the United States and Canada.

The following criteria were used to exclude materials from the *Bibliography*:

* Materials dealing with facility planning, design and evaluation, but not specifically with libraries.
* Materials focusing on equipment, such as office equipment, microform readers, computer terminals, fire protection equipment and electronic security equipment.
* Very short announcements of new or renovated facilities.
* Nonprint source materials other than microforms.
* Case studies and evaluations of existing or planned facilities. These make up a large portion of the literature and it was not practical to include all of them in the *Bibliography.* Those that are included should be seen as representative of their type, rather than a comprehensive collection of such items. In general, items were selected for inclusion based on some unusual or interesting feature of the described facility.
* Materials dealing with topics judged to have been adequately covered by other items in the *Bibliography.*

ARRANGEMENT

The *Bibliography* is divided into three major sections, each of which is further subdivided into additional sub-sections. All entries are arranged alphabetically by title within their respective sub-sections. When two items have the same title they are sub-ordered by the author's last name and the date of publication. Each entry has an item number which is assigned consecutively from 1 to 800 throughout the *Bibliography*.

The Table of Contents is designed to provide a fairly broad level of subject access to the *Bibliography*. It should be noted that it is the norm, rather than the exception, for items to cover several different facility topics within a single article or book. Since each item is included only once in the *Bibliography*, the decision of where to place the item was based on either the predominant topic covered by the item (in the case of Section 1) or by selected special topics (in the case of Sections 2 and 3). Additional subject retrieval can be achieved by using the subject index. The author index includes entries for all the first and second authors, editors, translators and compilers mentioned either in a full bibliographic citation or within an annotation.

Mary Sue Stephenson
School of Library, Archival and Information Studies
The University of British Columbia
Vancouver, British Columbia

1.0 FACILITY PLANNING, DESIGN, EVALUATION AND RENOVATION

1.1 General Overviews and Coverage of More Than One Type of Library

1.1.1 Bibliographies, Standards, History and Multiple-Library Statistical Overviews

1. *Administration, Personnel, Buildings and Equipment: A Handbook for Library Management,* by David F. Kohl. Santa Barbara: ABC Clio Information Services, 1985.

> Annotated bibliographic guide to the research literature of librarianship from 1960-1983. The chapter on buildings and equipment includes the topics audiovisual, automation, carrels, comfort, general equipment, handicapped needs, microforms, parking, physical layout, space needs, stacks, storage costs and terminals. Each section is subdivided by type of library.

2. *ALA World Encyclopedia of Library and Information Services,* edited by Robert Wedgeworth, et al. 2nd ed. Chicago: American Library Association, 1986.

> Several articles address facilities related concerns. Includes tables, illustrations and bibliographies.

3. *American Library Development, 1600-1899,* by Elizabeth W. Stone. New York: H.W. Wilson, 1977.

> A chronology of American library history, including coverage of library buildings. Includes an extensive bibliography.

4. *ARBA Guide to Library Science Literature, 1970-1983,* edited by Donald D. Davis, Jr. and Charles D. Patterson. Littleton: Libraries Unlimited, 1987.

> This critical annotated bibliography includes a chapter on architecture, facilities and equipment.

5. "Baroque Monastic Library Architecture," by Rolf Achilles. *Journal of Library History* 11(1976): 249-255.

> Reviews the architectural design of monastic libraries between 1580 and 1775. Includes photographs and a bibliography.

6. "Bibliography on Some Recent Materials on Building and Construction," by Stanley Adams. *Illinois Libraries* 69(1987): 625-628.

> Selected annotated bibliography. Topics covered include standards, guidelines and requirements, preservation, the planning and design process, evaluating facilities and financial factors.

7. "Building or Renovating Libraries: A Bibliography of Government Documents," by Kathleen Eisenbeis and Carson Holloway. *North Carolina Libraries* 39(1981): 42-48.

> Selective bibliography of U.S. government (federal and state) documents concerned with library design. Includes handicapped accessibility, historical renovation, energy and general information.

8. "Buildings, Library," by H.B. Schell. *Encyclopedia of Library and Information Science,* edited by Allen Kent, et al. New York: Marcel Dekker, 1968- (continuing).

> Broad overview of the development of library building design. Looks at historical evolution of building shapes, layouts, and current and future trends. Includes photographs, layouts and a bibliography.

9. "Canadian Library Buildings: Historical Perspective and Current Scene," by R. Gerald Prodrick. *Canadian Library Journal* 39(1982): 199-201.

> Reviews the development of Canadian library buildings since the 1700's, with an emphasis on facilities built since 1960. Two tables provide data on recently completed projects or those in progress at the time of publication.

10. *Encyclopedia of Library and Information Science,* edited by Allen Kent, et al. New York: Marcel Dekker, 1968- (continuing).

> Several articles cover a variety of facilities related topics, including for example, "Architecture, library building," and "buildings, library." Includes tables, illustrations and bibliographies.

11. "Facilities: Library Buildings," by A. Robert Rogers. *A Century of Service: Librarianship in the United States and Canada,* edited by Sidney L. Jackson, et al. Chicago: American Library Association, 1976. 221-242.

> Reviews the history of library architecture between 1876 and 1976. Includes an extensive bibliography.

12. *A History of Building Types,* by Nikolaus Pevsner. Princeton: Princeton University Press, 1976.

Includes chapter on the history of library buildings in
the West, beginning with the Alexandria Library and
ending with Philip Johnson's addition to the Boston
Public Library. Contains numerous photographs,
illustrations and an extensive bibliography.

13. *The Influence of Angus Snead Macdonald and the Snead
Bookstack on Library Architecture*, by Charles H. Baumann.
Metuchen: Scarecrow Press, 1972.

Reviews the historical development of the American
library building to 1941, followed by a detailed
discussion of Macdonald's role in the development of
library architecture and bookstacks. Includes floor plans,
a library building survey of 1930-1960, a list of Snead
and Company bookstack installations, photographs, and
an extensive bibliography.

14. "Library Buildings," by Walter C. Allen. *Library Trends*
25(1976): 89-112.

Reviews the architectural development of libraries during
the past 100 years, by examining the ways in which
changes in library functions and roles have been
reflected in facility design, the evolution of building
techniques and materials, aesthetic changes and the
impact of different financial environments. Includes a
bibliography.

15. "Library Buildings," by David Kaser. *ALA World
Encyclopedia of Library and Information Services*. 2nd ed.
1986.

Broad overview article on the history and design,
planning and construction, and general design
considerations of library buildings. Includes illustrations
and a bibliography.

16. "Library Buildings and Equipment: Sources of

Information," by A. Robert Rogers. *Library Journal* 97(1972): 3876-3877.

> Discusses sources of information on library facility design, including Library of Congress subject headings, standards and specifications, the indexing and abstracting literature, major monographs, journal articles, etc.

17. *Library Science Annual: Volume 1, 1985,* edited by Bohdan S. Wynar. Littleton: Libraries Unlimited, 1985.

> This evaluative annotated bibliography of books is a companion volume to American Reference Books Annual, and is to be issued annually beginning with this volume. Citations to facility planning and design items are not grouped together, but are instead found under a number of headings such as science and technology libraries, medical libraries, school library media centers, security, etc.

18. *McKim, Mead and White: Architects,* by R.G Wilson. New York: Rizzoli, 1983.

> Provides descriptions for many of the firm's most famous buildings, including those at Columbia University and the Boston Public Library. Includes numerous photographs and an extensive bibliography.

19. "The Origin and Evolution of Architectural Form of Roman Library," by Elizbieta Makowiecka. *Studia Antiqua* (1978): 5-109.

> Historical overview of ancient Greek and Roman library architecture. Includes photographs, site and schematic plans and an extensive bibliography.

20. *Reference Sources in Library and Information Services,* by Gary R. Purcell, with Gail A. Schlachter. Santa Barbara:

ABC Clio Information Services, 1984.

> This very extensive annotated bibliography includes numerous section headings which contain items dealing with facility planning and design, including the heading "building" and headings for specific types of libraries and materials.

21. "Selected References," by Walter C. Allen. *Library Trends* 36(1987): 475-491.

> Part of a special issue on library buildings, this non-annotated bibliography is divided into the categories bibliography, history and background, general, the planning team, the building program, alternatives to a new building, academic libraries, public libraries, school libraries, special libraries, site selection, maintenance, security, moving, interior planning, and furniture and equipment.

22. "Sources for the Study of American Library Architecture," Donald E. Oehlerts. *Journal of Library History* 11(1976): 68-78.

> Bibliographic essay reviewing the available sources for study of United States library architecture. Includes an extensive bibliography.

23. "Standards and Specifications for Library Buildings: A Comparative Analysis," by Rajwant Singh. *Lucknow Librarian* 15.2(1983): 65-73.

> Describes efforts made toward the development of facility design standards and specifications in India, together with a comparison of the resulting standards and their counterparts in other countries. Includes tables and a brief bibliography.

24. "Standards for Library Building," Franz Kroller. *Inspel*

16.1(1982): 40-44.

Reviews the efforts of the International Federation of Library Associations and Institutions (IFLA) to identify library building standards from around the world, and to create appropriate international standards.

1.1.2 Planning A Facility: General Considerations

25. "An Aid to Library Planning," Michael Dewe. *Assistant Librarian* 70(1977): 156-157.

Describes the benefits of using layout planning kits when designing a new layout or redesigning an old one.

26. "Analyzing Architectural and Interior Design Plans," by Elaine Cohen. *Library Administration and Management* 1(1987): 91-93.

Recommends using the library service policy as the basis for the architectural and interior design of libraries, with aesthetics taking a lower priority than the practical needs of the institution. Suggests using computer-aided design software and bubble diagrams as planning aids. Includes examples of schematic and layout drawings.

27. "The Architect," by Bud Oringdulph. *Talking Buildings: A Practical Dialogue on Programming and Planning Library Buildings,* edited by Raymond M. Holt. Proceedings of a Building Workshop, Pasadena, California, October 3-4, 1985. Sacramento: California State Library, 1986. 23-33. ERIC ED 271109.

Outlines the role of the architect and architect's team in the facility planning process and provides guidelines to use when selecting an architect. Also reviews other possible members of the team such as engineers, specialists, consultants and the interior designer. Looks at the role of the architects in each of the basic phases of the planning and construction process. Also briefly considers the librarian's role and responsibilities.

28. "The Architect as Library Planner," by Mark Mitchell. *Library Space Planning: Issues and Approaches* (*LJ* Special Report no. 1, edited by Karl Nyren) New York: R.R. Bowker, 1976. 65-70.

Describes a planning and design approach in which the architect works very closely with the library staff. Suggests the necessity of organizing architectural elements into groupings of interrelated staff and functions. Also considers the factor of cost and provides a sample cost chart comparing a new building and a renovation.

29. "Architects' Fees: Their Place in Library Planning," by Jerrold Orne. *Library Journal* 95(1970): 4135-4141.

Provides an overview of the architectural fee process, including a review of several American Institute of Architects' publications. Also reports results of a survey of architects and librarians on the fee practices in their states. Includes table organized by state showing cost schedules of typical architects' fees.

30. "Architectural Approaches to Design and Behavior," by Nancy McAdams. *The User Encounters the Library: An Interdisciplinary Focus on the User/System Interface*, edited by Martin B. Steffenson and Larry D. Larason. Proceedings of a Library Training Institute, Monroe, Louisiana, July 31-August 3, 1978. Monroe: Northeast Louisiana University, 1986. 1-9. ERIC ED 266791.

Reviews the architectural and building program process. Emphasizes the roles and interaction of the architect and the user (the library) in the design process.

Examines acoustics, environmental control, space requirements, growth requirements, lighting and how standards and formulas are used.

31. "Assembling Dreams and Reality: The Job of the Library Building Consultant," by Mary H. Zenke. *Illinois Libraries* 67(1985): 792-794.

Looks at the role of the building consultant. Topics covered include finding the right consultant, interviewing and hiring, selecting and working with the architect, the building program statement, and other duties or services provided by the consultant.

32. "Building a Library: The Librarian/Architect Relationship," by R.E. Carroll. *New Zealand Libraries* 45.5(1987): 85-89.

Describes the roles of the librarian and the architect in library planning, with emphasis on the importance of establishing a strong relationship.

33. "Building a Solid Architect-Client Relationship," by Matthew J. Simon and George Yourke. *Library Administration and Management* 1(1987): 100-103.

Stresses the importance of developing strong relationships between the architects and the librarian, and defines their individual roles. Includes table which separates the responsibilities for different stages of the planning, design and construction process.

34. *Building Codes and Regulations,* by John L. Fisher. Paper presented at the American Library Association Annual Conference, 94th, San Francisco, June 29-July 5, 1975. ERIC ED 111372.

Discusses how building codes and standards can provide librarians and architects with guidelines leading to the prevention of fires. Provides overview of major building code information bodies, as well as those formulating standards.

35. "Building + People + Activity," by Richard T. Santos. *California Librarian* 34(1975): 28-39.

Reports results of a survey 117 libraries by an architectural firm. Includes such factors as acoustics, lighting, air conditioning, fire, vandalism, adequacy of space for various functional areas, problems with the programming process and problems with contracts, architects, and site planning.

36. "Building Program Check List." *Illinois Libraries* 69(1987): 675-676.

Provides checklist of the planning, design and construction process.

37. "The Building Program: Generalities," by George J. Snowball. *Planning Library Buildings: From Decision to Design*, edited by Lester K. Smith. Papers from a Preconference at the 1984 American Library Association Annual Conference, Dallas, Texas. Chicago: Library Administration and Management Association, American Library Association, 1986. 71-82.

Overview of the purposes, design and use of a formal building program. Topics covered include definitions, intended audience, importance in the planning process, who should write the program, content, priorities and the line between planning and designing. Includes a bibliography.

38. *Buildings for the Arts*, by Jeremy Robinson and Martin Filler. (An *Architectural Record* book) New York: McGraw-Hill, 1978.

Provides detailed architectural data, floor plans, and

illustrations of different types of arts-related facilities. Includes chapter on libraries.

39. "Color and Lighting in the Library," by Marjorie McCarthy. *NNCL* (*News Notes of California Libraries*) 65(1970): 494-502.

Discusses use of color in libraries in terms of overall architectural design factors such as program, site, climate, orientation, light and materials.

40. *Combining Libraries: The Canadian and Australian Experience*, edited by L.J. Amey. (The Dalhousie University School of Library and Information Studies Series, no. 2) Metuchen: Scarecrow Press, 1987.

Presents the experiences of librarians, administrators and supervisors in Canada and Australia who have participated in the process of combining and using school and public library facilities. Includes illustrations, a sample evaluation scheme, state and provincial guidelines, and a very extensive international bibliography.

41. "Communicating With Graphics in the Library Building Program," by Richard B. Hall. *Illinois Libraries* 67(1985): 777-786.

Discusses the enhancement of the overall facility programming process and the building program document preparation through the appropriate use of graphics and text. "Space Data Sheets" are explained and the purpose of each section is covered. Also discusses "Divisional Data Sheets," divisional spatial diagrams, and master spatial diagrams, including the use of axonometric views. Includes tables and illustrations.

42. "Communication Between the Architect and the

Librarian," by Abdullahi Mohammed. *Pakistan Library Bulletin* 12.3-4(1981): 17-19.

> Looks at the importance of establishing good relations and trust between the librarian and the architect.

43. "Construction Cost Estimating and Project Cash Flow," by Bud Oringdulph. *Talking Buildings: A Practical Dialogue on Programming and Planning Library Buildings*, edited by Raymond M. Holt. Proceedings of a Building Workshop, Pasadena, California, October 3-4, 1985. Sacramento: California State Library, 1986. 117-127. ERIC ED 271109.

> Overview of the role of construction costs in the building project. Topics covered include published construction cost indexes/trends, converting net to gross square feet, locality adjustments, cost evaluation during design and cash flow. Includes figures showing how cost estimates are organized, cost estimation components, project cost summary, sample of component estimation, design development estimate, quantitative takeoff cost estimate and final cost estimate summary.

44. "The Contract Documents and Final Working Papers," by Charles R. Smith. *Planning Library Buildings: From Decision to Design*, edited by Lester K. Smith. Papers from a Preconference at the 1984 American Library Association Annual Conference, Dallas, Texas. Chicago: Library Administration and Management Association, American Library Association, 1986. 141-152.

> Looks at the different types of documents which make up the contracts used in planning and constructing a new building. Topics covered include definitions of common terms, working drawings, specifications, instructions to bidders, general and supplementary conditions and the owner-contractor agreement. Also describes how to read and interpret working drawings and includes five sample drawings.

45. "The Design/Build Alternative," by Gloria J. Novak. *Planning Library Buildings: From Decision to Design,* edited by Lester K. Smith. Papers from a Preconference at the 1984 American Library Association Annual Conference, Dallas, Texas. Chicago: Library Administration and Management Association, American Library Association, 1986. 175-188.

> Discusses a design approach where the library provides a budget and a building program to a partnership made up of the architect and the contractor. This approach is contrasted with the traditional method where the architect completes the drawings and specifications before the construction contracts are let using the bidding process. Topics covered include the basic design/build process, the building program, performance specifications, selection of the design/build entity and problems with the approach. Also briefly looks at how this approach was used to plan and construct the Dallas Public Library, the University of Denver library and the University of California at Berkeley library.

46. "The Design of Library Buildings in Southeast Asia with Special Reference to National and University Libraries," by Halimah B. Zaman. Dissertation. Loughborough University of Technology, 1980.

> Reviews the major factors which have impacted library building design and construction in recent years and will continue to do so in the future. Discusses the importance of using well established design principles and proposes such a set of such principles for academic and national library buildings. Includes tables, illustrations and a bibliography.

47. "Design Today," by Andrea Michaels. *Wilson Library Bulletin* 62.5(1987): 50-51.

> Provides a two page checklist to be used when critically evaluating a facility. Areas covered include site

and structural, architectural, access, storage, electrical/data/communication cabling, telephones, mechanical, fire protection, finishes, major areas, special areas, signage, service points, display, and things to avoid.

48. "Designed for Users," by Nolan Lushington. *Wilson Library Bulletin* 57.2(1982): 148-151.

Discusses the importance of communicating to the architect the unique aspects of a particular library environment before the building is designed. Topics covered include the relationships of users to the design and layout, reference and information areas, lighting, temperature and environmental control, load bearing floors, ease of access to collection, signage and graphics, location of telephone reference, electrical power system, group usage areas and multipurpose rooms, lounge areas and children's areas.

49. *Designing and Space Planning for Libraries: A Behavioral Guide,* by Aaron Cohen and Elaine Cohen. New York: R.R. Bowker, 1979.

This work stresses the use of behavioral theory and techniques when building or remodeling library facilities. Within this framework, topics covered include the planning process, the planning team, fees, acoustics, mechanical systems, energy concerns, and space organization and allocation. Includes tables, illustrations and a bibliography.

50. "Designing Libraries to Sell Services," by Elaine Cohen. *Wilson Library Bulletin* 55(1980): 190-195.

Author advocates the utilization of effective and creative design as a means of attracting users to the library, including entrances, space usage, seating and flexible design to allow for technological changes.

51. "Designing Tomorrow's Libraries," by Carlton C. Rochell. *Architectural Record* 171(1983): 91.

> Discusses possible future trends in society that will impact the design of public and academic library facilities, including computers, the reduction of space required to house collections and the concept of "information rich vs. information poor".

52. "A Dozen Ways to Make Your Architect Love You," by Marilyn Hawkins. *Technicalities* 3.3(1983): 5,11.

> Guidelines for creating and sustaining a successful relationship between the library and the architect.

53. "Equipment, Furniture and Modular Planning," by Keyes D. Metcalf. *Colloquium on University Library · Buildings*, edited by K.W. Humphreys. Special issue of *LIBER Bulletin*, Supplement Number 1, 1972: 40-56.

> Reviews the use of modular building design in relation to furniture and equipment layouts, including both the problems and advantages of this design approach. Looks at bay sizes, column spacing and size. Provides questions and guidelines for determining optimal modular arrangement and components. Includes layout drawings of differently sized bays.

54. "Estimating Library Building Project Costs at an Early Stage," by David Sabsay. *Talking Buildings: A Practical Dialogue on Programming and Planning Library Buildings*, edited by Raymond M. Holt. Proceedings of a Building Workshop, Pasadena, California, October 3-4, 1985. Sacramento: California State Library, 1986. 93-102. ERIC ED 271109.

> Reviews cost estimation process for site acquisition, construction contracts, furniture and equipment, other costs, and contingency costs. Includes sample library building project budget.

55. "Field/Performance Theory Applied to Library Space Planning," by Meredith Bloss. *Library Space Planning: Issues and Approaches (LJ* Special Report no. 1, edited by Karl Nyren) New York: R.R. Bowker, 1976. 52-54.

> Describes how the field theory and the performance theory of library planning can be used to relate the actual requirements of specific library patrons and programs to space planning, rather than through the use of generalized standards and guidelines.

56. "Financing Library Construction," by Bertha D. Hellum. *California Librarian* 31(1970): 52-57.

> Reviews several aspects of public library construction financing, including determining adequate space requirements, costs of space and means of financing construction.

57. "Finding Your Way Through Drawings and Specifications," by Bud Oringdulph. *Talking Buildings: A Practical Dialogue on Programming and Planning Library Buildings*, edited by Raymond M. Holt. Proceedings of a Building Workshop, Pasadena, California, October 3-4, 1985. Sacramento: California State Library, 1986. 155-172. ERIC ED 271109.

> Explains how to read and interpret architectural drawings and specifications, including construction drawings, site plans, floor plans, elevation drawings, component drawings, and structural, mechanical and electrical drawings. Includes illustrations of several different types of drawings and specifications.

58. *The How-to-Do-It Manual for Small Libraries*, edited by Bill Katz. New York: Neal-Schuman, 1987.

> Aimed at small academic, public and special libraries, this work includes coverage of the planning and management of library facilities. Includes a bibliography.

59. "Ideals and Axioms: Library Architecture," by Jane Holtz Kay. *American Libraries* 5(1974): 240-246.

> Overview essay of the role architecture plays in how libraries are perceived and used. Includes photographs.

60. "The Influence of Architecture on People: A Theoretical View with Reference to Libraries," by E.A. Mare. *South African Journal of Library and Information Science* 55.2(1987): 94-105.

> Examines the theoretical, psychological and practical ways in which people react to library facilities. Includes recommendations for library designers.

61. "The Influence of Library Interior on Library Use," by Bent Nilsson and Hans Lembol. *Round Table of National Centers for Library Services* 1(1985): 6-10.

> Looks at design factors which can affect the view of the library by the user, including architecture, layout, furniture, color, lighting, and signage.

62. "Interaction of Building, Functions and Management," by Margaret Beckman. *Canadian Library Journal* 39(1982): 203-205.

> Discusses the conceptual relationships of buildings, library functions and library management, and the influence of these factors on facility design. Includes photograph, floor plan, and functional relationship table.

63. *Libraries: A Briefing and Design Guide,* edited by Allen Konya. London: The Architectural Press, 1986.

> Very detailed examination at the process used to develop and implement the library building program (brief). Topics covered include preparing the preliminary brief, the initial brief, feasibility, the detailed brief,

outline proposals and scheme design, siting, design and construction methods and major participants in the process. Includes numerous illustrations, photographs, spatial relationship (bubble) diagrams, tables, and an annotated bibliography.

64. *Libraries: Architecture and Equipment,* by Michael Browne. New York: Praeger, 1970.

Bilingual (English and German) overview of library facility planning and design. Topics covered include historical review of library architecture and design, the library building and types of libraries, the functional components of the library, and the impact of growth and change. Includes numerous photographs, floor plans, and descriptions of specific libraries, photographs and tables related to functional areas and furnishings, and a bibliography.

65. "The Library Building Consultant and the Library Planning Team," by Margaret Beckman. *Planning Library Buildings: From Decision to Design,* edited by Lester K. Smith. Papers from a Preconference at the 1984 American Library Association Annual Conference, Dallas, Texas. Chicago: Library Administration and Management Association, American Library Association, 1986. 57-68.

Reviews the basic purposes and responsibilities of consultants used during the planning process. Topics covered include reasons to use consultants, types of consultants, how and when to choose a consultant, formalizing the arrangement, paying the consultant and responsibilities.

66. *Library Building: Innovation for Changing Needs,* edited by Alphonse F. Trezza. Proceedings of the Library Buildings Institute conducted at San Francisco, California, June 22-24, 1967. Chicago: American Library Association, 1972.

Overview of planning for technological innovation in

library facilities and general planning issues. Includes the following papers which are not treated separately in this bibliography since they were given before 1970, "How library automation may influence new building plans," by Joseph Becker, "Building-planning implications of automation," by Robert R. McClarren, "Why a building program," by Robert H. Rohlf, "Who prepares the program statement," by Margaret K. Troke, "What goes into a building program," by Robert E. Thomas, "Elementary notes on site selection," by Julius Chitwood, "On location of library buildings," by Theodore S. Hills, "The librarian's role," by Edward C. Perry, "The architect's role," by Eugene W. Fickes, "The consultant's role," by Robert H. Rohlf, "The governmental authority," by Martin D. Phelan, "Federal financial assistance," by Robert R. McClarren, "Library bond issues," by Albert C. Lake, "Lesser-known financing methods," by Julius Chitwood, "The new curriculum and its implications for the IMC," by John Goodlad, "New technological developments applicable to the IMC," by Philip Lewis, "Planning for the individual utilization of resources: an illustrated overview," by Boyd M. Bolvin, "Materials production area in the new IMC," by Jerrold E. Kemp, "Educational needs and remodeling the instructional materials center," by John Church, "The viewpoint of the building specialist," by Robert Hull, "Case studies of remodeling in California schools," by Helen Cyr, et al., "The administrator's role," by Gene L. Schwilck, "The role of other key personnel," by Howard Sagehorn and Arden Smith, "Designs for correctional libraries," by Robert J. Brooks, "The importance of good physical facilities," by A. Dal Favero, "Impact of automation on library building design," by Chris G. Stevenson, and "A regional architect looks at the library," by Ralph Askin.

67. "The Library Building Program: Key to Success," by Lance C. Finney. *Public Libraries* 23.3(1984): 79-81.

Reviews the importance of the building program in the facility design process and in the overall administration of the library. Includes outline of recommended components of program statement.

68. "Library Buildings," edited by Anders C. Dahlgren. *Library Trends* 36(1987): 261-491.

Special issue on library buildings. Includes the following articles which are treated separately in this bibliography, "Trends in public library buildings," by Raymond M. Holt, "Trends in academic library facilities," by Nancy R. McAdams, "Trends in special library buildings," by Elaine Cohen and Aaron Cohen, "Trends in school library media facilities, furnishings, and collections," by Jim Bennett, "On the verge of a revolution: current trends in library lighting," by Bradley A. Waters and Willis C. Winters, "Mechanical systems and libraries," by Fred Dubin, "Toward the environmental design of library buildings," by Lamar Veatch, "Trends in staff furnishings for libraries," by John Vasi, "Output measures and library space planning," by Nolan Lushington, "Alternatives to the construction of a new library," by B. Franklin Hemphill, "Reutilizing existing library space," by Marlys Cresap Davis, "Trends in financing public library buildings," by Richard B. Hall, "The library building tomorrow," by Richard L. Waters, and "Selected References," by Walter C. Allen.

69. "Library Buildings: Basic Principles and Primary Elements of Design," by Akhtar Hanif. *Pakistan Library Bulletin* 9.1-2(1978): 6-16.

Overview of the basic principles and factors involved in planning, designing, and constructing a library building. Advocates the position that the basic principles and process is the same for all types of libraries. Includes a bibliography.

70. *Library Buildings Consultant List.* Building and Equipment Section, Library Administration and Management Association. Chicago: American Library Association, 1976- . (Irregular).

List of individuals who meet the minimum qualifications for building consultants established by ALA. The entry for each person includes name, address, current affiliation, library school, experience during the last ten years (number of projects, size of projects in square feet), total number of years of building consultant experience, type of library building projects preferred, five most recent library building projects, type of project expertise, type of services offered, geographical limitation, availability, and fees.

71. "Library Buildings: The Modular Design," by Marcia de Steuben. *Current Studies in Librarianship* 8.1/2(1984): 28-34.

Reviews the application of modular architecture and design to library buildings. Looks at advantages and disadvantages of the modular approach and how it compares with fixed design buildings. Includes a bibliography.

72. "Library Design and Planning in Developing Countries," by P. Havard-Williams and J.E. Jengo. *Libri* 37.2(1987): 160-176.

Reviews the major planning and construction considerations of building a library facility in third world countries. Topics covered include the roles of the librarian and the architect, consultants, building for the specific climatic conditions, and furniture. Includes a bibliography.

73. "Library Design for Today's User," by Philip R. Brook. *Canadian Architect* 23(1978): 30-35.

Presented from an architect's point of view, this article discusses how librarians and architects should attempt to share their views and opinions on facility design.

74. "Library Designs, What Not To Do: Successful Library

Building Programs Avoid These Common Pitfalls," by Robert H. Rohlf. *American Libraries* 17(1986): 100-104.

> Discusses problems associated with the concept "form follows function." Topics covered include the potential danger of architectural drama and elements, communications difficulties between the librarian and the architect, authority relationships, problems of planning by committee, reviewing the building program, lighting, setting and meeting schedules, furniture and equipment and construction problems.

75. *Library Interior Layout and Design,* by Rolf Fuhlrott and Michael Dewe. Proceedings of the Seminar Held in Frederiksdal, Denmark, June 16-20, 1980. (IFLA Publication 24) New York: K.G. Saur, 1982.

> Overview of library facility planning, largely from a European perspective. The following papers are treated separately in this bibliography, "Library buildings in Denmark," by Sven Plougaard, "The planning of public libraries in Denmark," by Elisabeth Lylloff, "Energy savings in the planning of library buildings," by Franz Kroller, "Physical conditions and their influence on library layout and design," by J. Boot, "Graphic design in libraries," by Povl Abrahamsen, and "On library lighting," by Rolf Fuhlrott. Includes a bibliography.

76. *Library Space Planning,* by Ruth A. Fraley and Carol Lee Anderson. New York: Neal-Schuman, 1985.

> A broad overview of library space planning, this books looks at the topics of goals and objectives, financial considerations, the bid process, personnel, safety, shelving and storage, and moving. Includes illustrations and a bibliography.

77. "Library Space Planning for the Years Ahead," by Jerrold Orne. *Library Space Planning: Issues and Approaches,* (*LJ* Special Report no. 1, edited by Karl Nyren) New York:

R.R. Bowker, 1976. 2-4.

Reviews expected changes in library design and space planning during the next ten years. Identified areas of concern include architecture, audiovisual materials, electronic technology, networks, reference and research function, institutional planning, restricted access and engineering.

78. *Library Space Planning: Issues and Approaches*, edited by Karl Nyren. (*LJ* Special Report no. 1) New York: R.R. Bowker, 1976.

Overview of the library space planning process. Includes the following papers which are treated separately in this bibliography: "Library space planning for the years ahead," by John F. Anderson, "The second generation store front library," by B.F. Hemphill, "Space planning for community information services," by Robert Croneberger, Jr. and Carolyn Luck, "The information center library," by Nolan Lushington, "A public library site symposium," by Hoyt R. Galvin, "Factors in space planning for the learning resource center," by Joleen Bock, "User environment in a microform center," by Arthur Tannenbaum and Eva Sidhom, "Saving space, energy and money with mobile compact shelving: Georgetown University," by Joseph E. Jeffs, "The failure of the divisional plan at Drake," by Thomas P. Slavens, "Field/Performance theory applied to library space planning," by Meredith Bloss, "Gaining space by creative re-arrangement of library areas," by Rolf Myller, "Do our library buildings have to be discarded every fifteen years?" by Elaine Cohen and Aaron Cohen, "Addition, remodeling, renovation projects," by Hoyt. R. Galvin, "Energy conservation and library design," by William C. Tippens, "The architect as library planner," by Mark Mitchell and "The planning team," by Hoyt R. Galvin.

79. "Management Styles and Techniques: Space," by Dale S. Montanelli, et al. *Illinois Libraries* 69(1987): 130-142.

Consists of two short articles. The first deals with
space management in general and the second looks at
how to successfully design and implement a successful
space management plan.

80. "A Menu for Building Programs," by Raymond M. Holt.
*Talking Buildings: A Practical Dialogue on Programming and
Planning Library Buildings.* Edited by Raymond M. Holt.
Proceedings of a Building Workshop, Pasadena, California,
October 3-4, 1985. Sacramento: California State Library,
1986. 65-92. ERIC ED 271109.

Reviews in detail the rationale behind and overall
process of creating a successful building program. Topics
covered include the program's objectives, who prepares
the program, making space projections, using functional
relationships, narrative description of areas, technical
requirements and program format. Includes several
functional relationships diagrams.

81. "Merged Facilities: Potential and Constraints," by Mae
Graham and J. Maurice Travillan. *Media Center Facilities
Design,* compiled and edited by Jane A. Hannigan and Glenn
E. Estes. Chicago: American Library Association, 1978.
97-102.

Looks at the use of combined school and public library
facilities, including discussion of both the advantages
and disadvantages of the approach. Includes a
bibliography.

82. "Planning a Library in the Tropics," by Imelda B.
Cancio. *Bulletin of the Philippine Library Association*
13.1-4(1980-1981): 74-85.

Reviews the special factors which must be considered
when planning, designing, constructing and maintaining
a library facility in several varieties of tropical
climates. Includes floor plans and other illustrations.

83. "Planning Aids for a New Library Building." *Illinois Libraries* 67(1985): 794-808.

Reviews planning aids used in designing library facilities. Topics covered include building project sequence, program components, site selection and size of site for the public library, selection of the architect, effective space planning, floor loading factors, lighting, life cycle costing and value analysis, building energy management (a checklist for potential savings), planning for better maintenance, checklist for barrier free access, general planning data for shelving and seating, specifications for purchasing furniture and equipment and converting linear feet to square feet. Includes an extensive bibliography.

84. *Planning and Design of Library Buildings*, by Godfrey Thompson. 2nd ed. New York: Nichols Publishing, 1977.

Overview of British practice related to library facility design, covering all types of libraries.. Topics covered include planning and the program, the feasibility study, layouts and functional space requirements, furniture, floors, circulation, lighting, security, physical conditions, enclosing elements and finishes, design details and drawings and conversions. Appendices give published British standards, a network analysis for planning a university library, and a bibliography. Includes numerous photographs, charts, tables, floor plans, flow and functional diagrams, etc.

85. "Planning and Design of Library Buildings: The Indian Experience," by Girja Kumar. *Library Herald* 20.2-4(1981-1982): 59-72.

Reviews and contrasts Indian and Western experiences with library planning and design. Discusses problems associated with facility planning in India.

86. "Planning Library Buildings," by Margaret Beckman and

Stephan Langmead. *Canadian Library Journal* 28(1971): 114-120.

> Stresses the importance of the librarian being involved in planning a new facility. Also advocates the use of a building program committee to help write the program statement.

87. *Planning Library Buildings: From Decision to Design,* edited by Lester K. Smith. Papers from a Preconference at the American Library Association Annual Conference, Dallas, 1984. Chicago: Library Administration and Management Association, American Library Association, 1986.

> Includes 15 papers dealing with various aspects of library facility planning. The following are covered individually in this bibliography, "Needs assessment for academic libraries," by Bob Carmack, "Needs assessment, the point of origin," by Raymond M. Holt, "Planning teams for library buildings," by Gloria J. Novak, "The library building consultant and the library planning team," by Margaret Beckman, "Decision-making in academic library building planning," by Joel G. Clemmer, "The building program: generalities," by George J. Snowball, "Using functional relationships (bubble diagrams) in your building program," by Raymond M. Holt, "The role and selection of the architect," by Nancy R. McAdams, "Schematic design and design development," by Susan O'Brien, "The concept and schematics phase of preparing architectural drawings," by Richard L. Waters, "The contract documents and final working drawings," by Charles R. Smith, "Some added thoughts on final working documents," by Donald G. Kelsey, "Lighting and air conditioning in libraries," by Lester K. Smith, "The design/build alternative," by Gloria J. Novak and "Planning library buildings in other lands," by David Kaser.

88. "Planning Library Buildings in Other Lands," by Gloria J. Novak. *Planning Library Buildings: From Decision to*

Design, edited by Lester K. Smith. Papers from a Preconference at the 1984 American Library Association Annual Conference, Dallas, Texas. Chicago: Library Administration and Management Association, American Library Association, 1986. 189-192.

Discusses the difficulties of applying the experiences and lessons of American library design to other countries.

89. "Planning of a Library," by Michael G. Werleman and Jean-Eudes Guy. *Argus* 15.3(1986): 73-78.

Reviews the basic considerations relevant to planning and constructing a library building, using the perspective of basic architectural principles. Includes a bibliography.

90. "The Planning Team," by Hoyt R. Galvin. *Library Space Planning: Issues and Approaches* (*LJ* Special Report no. 1, edited by Karl Nyren) New York: R.R. Bowker, 1976. 74-77.

Discusses the roles in library facility design of the planning team, including the librarian, the architect, the building consultant and the interior planner.

91. "Planning Teams for Library Buildings," by Gloria J. Novak. *Planning Library Buildings: From Decision to Design,* edited by Lester K. Smith. Papers from a Preconference at the 1984 American Library Association Annual Conference, Dallas, Texas. Chicago: Library Administration and Management Association, American Library Association, 1986. 43-56.

Recommends the use of three different planning teams to work parallel during the planning process, with each responsible for different phases of the project. The three teams are the information-gathering, the major decision-making and the project planning. The paper discusses the members, roles and responsibilities of each team.

92. "Putting the Planning Team Together," by Nancy R. McAdams. *Talking Buildings: A Practical Dialogue on Programming and Planning Library Buildings*, edited by Raymond M. Holt. Proceedings of a Building Workshop, Pasadena, California, October 3-4, 1985. Sacramento: California State Library, 1986. 7-17. ERIC ED 271109.

> Reviews what members of the planning team do, who is responsible to whom, how each member is selected and during what stages of the process each participates. Includes figures showing responsibility relationships and participation by project phases. Also reviews selection of the architectural firm, the library consultant and the interior designer.

93. *Reader on the Library Building*, edited by Hal B. Schell. Englewood: Microcard Edition Books, 1975.

> Collection of 44 previously published articles dealing with library buildings. Since almost all were originally published before 1970, they are not treated separately in this bibliography. The articles are grouped into nine broad topics, including the past and future of library buildings, the use of consultants, the building program, site considerations, some general planning considerations, staff spaces, mechanical spaces, some considerations for newer media and automation services in the library building and furnishings and equipment. Includes illustrations (although not all illustrations from the original articles are included) and bibliographies.

94. "Ready, Willing, and Able: Preparing the Staff Team," by Ardenn Perkins, et al. *Illinois Libraries* 67(1985): 786-791.

> Part of a special issue on library buildings, this article discusses the membership of the building planning committee and the roles they play through the planning, construction and acceptance aspects of the process. Topics covered include the architect, responsibilities of the owner (library), responsibilities of

the board, the program, passing the referendum, assessing community needs and construction. Concludes with 13 item suggestion list of how process could be improved through more intense use of staff.

95. "Realities: Funding of Library Construction," by Kenneth E. Beasley. *Running Out of Space: What are the Alternatives?*, edited by Gloria Novak. Papers from a Preconference at the American Library Association Annual Meeting, 1975. Chicago: American Library Association, 1978. 121-136.

Reviews the problems associated with acquiring adequate funding for library construction or renovation, including future trends likely to impact facility requirements. Includes discussion by participants at the preconference.

96. "The Role and Selection of the Architect," by Nancy R. McAdams. *Planning Library Buildings: From Decision to Design*, edited by Lester K. Smith. Papers from a Preconference at the 1984 American Library Association Annual Conference, Dallas, Texas. Chicago: Library Administration and Management Association, American Library Association, 1986. 107-118.

This paper provides an overview of the topic, including the role of the architect, scope of architectural services and selection of the architectural firm. Includes a bibliography and a list of documents distributed by the American Institute of Architects that deal with the use of architects.

97. "Schematic Design and Design Development," by Susan O'Brien. *Planning Library Buildings: From Decision to Design*, edited by Lester K. Smith. Papers from a Preconference at the 1984 American Library Association Annual Conference, Dallas Texas. Chicago: Library Administration and Management Association, American Library Association, 1986. 119-132.

Reviews what schematics are and how they are utilized during the facility design project. Looks at why schematics are used, how to read them, the relationship to conceptual design, design development and schematic design and the relationship of schematics to the contracts.

98. *Scientific and Technical Libraries* by Nancy J. Pruett. 2 vol. Orlando: Academic Press, 1986.

As part of a very detailed examination of the functions, management and organization of scientific and technical libraries, this work contains a chapter on space planning. Includes illustrations and a bibliography.

99. "Seminar on New Problems in Library Architecture." *LIBER Bulletin* 16(1981): 1-94. Proceedings of a Seminar held in Heidelberg, November, 1980.

Includes 13 papers on different aspects of library building architecture, planning and design. Papers are in English, French, or German. Includes tables, illustrations, and bibliographies.

100. "Some Added Thoughts on Final Working Drawings," by Donald G. Kelsey. *Planning Library Buildings: From Decision to Design*, edited by Lester K. Smith. Papers from a Preconference at the 1984 American Library Association Annual Conference, Dallas, Texas. Chicago: Library Administration and Management Association, American Library Association, 1986. 153-162.

Looks at the purposes of final working drawings, including architectural drawings, structural drawings, mechanical drawings and electrical drawings.

101. "Spaces, Planning, and Etc.," by Martin Van Buren. *Library Space Planning: Issues and Approaches* (*LJ* Special Report no. 1, edited by Karl Nyren) New York: R.R.

Bowker, 1976. 71-73.

Library consultant's list of common problems encountered in library facility planning. Includes conflicts between architects and librarians, funding the furnishings budget, influences of personal prejudice and responsibility and authority of the planning team.

102. "Speaking of Responsibilities: You the Client," by Raymond M. Holt. *Talking Buildings: A Practical Dialogue on Programming and Planning Library Buildings*, edited by Raymond Holt. Proceedings of a Building Workshop, Pasadena, California, October 3-4, 1985. Sacramento: California State Library, 1986. 173-181. ERIC ED 271109.

Reviews role of the library and librarian in the library building program process. Topics covered include assembling and providing accurate information, selection of team members, contract administration, effective use of project team time, location of team meetings, timely response for information and review, understanding contract provisions, saving money for "extras," staff participation and internal communications.

103. "Special Report: How to Work With An Architect," by Myron E. Lewis and Mark L. Nelson. *Wilson Library Bulletin* 57.1(1982): 44-46.

Discusses how to select an architect. Also covers the services an architect can provide, including guidance on site selection, budgeting, project time lines, planning for the future, preparing the program, preparation of drawings and helping the library sell the project. Briefly looks at common areas of disagreement between architects and librarians.

104. "Special Report: Opening Day, What to Expect in a New Library," by Daniel Suvak. *Wilson Library Bulletin* 57.2(1982): 140-141, 190.

Describes the process of opening a new library or renovation, including such factors as staff orientation, satisfying users during the move, preparing for increased activity, adequate parking, providing quiet study spaces, security and evaluation.

105. "Structural Requirements of Library Building," by Robert M. Beder. *Planning the Special Library*, edited by Ellis Mount. (SLA Monograph no. 4) New York: Special Libraries Association, 1972. 13-17.

Reviews the structural considerations related to building a library facility. Topics covered include modular design, ventilation, lighting, power, acoustics, floors, walls and ceilings.

106. *Talking Buildings: A Practical Dialogue on Programming and Planning Library Buildings*, edited by Raymond M. Holt. Proceedings of a Building Workshop, Pasadena, California, October 3-4, 1985. Sacramento: California State Library, 1986. ERIC ED 271109.

Includes the following papers which are treated separately in this bibliography: "Putting the planning team together, " by Nancy R. McAdams, "Putting together the planning team - case study of the architect selection process," by Jane E. Light, "The architect," by Bud Oringdulph, "The interior designer," by Marshall Brown, "Turning needs into space requirements," by Nancy R. McAdams, "Turning needs into space requirements: the public library," by Raymond M. Holt, "Establishing library building costs at an early stage," by David Sabsay, "Questions about LSCA Title II," by Cy Silver, "Converting program to costs and costs to funding academic libraries," by Nancy R. McAdams, "Construction cost estimating and project cash flow," by Bud Oringdulph, "Interior planning for an integrated whole," by Marshall Brown, "Hermit crab buildings: living in someone else's shell," by Bud Oringdulph, "Finding your way through drawings and specifications," by Bud Oringdulph and

"Speaking of responsibilities," by Raymond M. Holt. Includes extensive bibliographies, sample planning documents, appendix on site selection, formulas, standards and guidelines, "Library Facility Scorecard," building program outline for public libraries, parking guidelines, ergonomic guidelines appendix on flexible work spaces and list of academic library building projects.

107. *Tropical Librarianship,* by Wilfred J. Plumbe. Metuchen: Scarecrow Press, 1987.

Detailed examination of the special problems and concerns associated with planning and managing libraries in tropical climates, including planning library facilities, choosing furniture and equipment, facilities and materials preservation.

108. "Update if You're Out of Date," by Richard J. Wolfert. *Wisconsin Library Bulletin* 71(1975): 201-202.

Stresses the importance of constantly reviewing and revising the library building program statement.

109. "The Use of Queuing Networks and Mixed Integer Programming to Allocate Resources Optimally Within a Library Layout," by J. Macgregor Smith. *Journal of the American Society for Information Science* 32(1981): 33-42.

Proposes modeling process to be used as part of the development of the building planning program and layout. Includes tables and a bibliography.

110. "Using Functional Relationships (Bubble Diagrams) in Your Building Program," by Raymond M. Holt. *Planning Library Buildings: From Decision to Design,* edited by Lester K. Smith. Papers from a Preconference at the 1984 American Library Association Annual Conference, Dallas, Texas. Chicago: Library Administration and Management

Association, American Library Association, 1986. 83-106.

> Detailed look at bubble diagrams and how they can be used to improve the building program document. Topics covered include definitions, creation of diagrams, interpretation of diagrams and creative aspects of the process. Includes ten sample bubble diagrams.

111. "The Whys and Hows of Writing a Library Building Program," by Leland M. Park. *The Library Scene* (1976): 2-5.

> Provides guidelines and checklist to use when preparing a library building program. Includes examples of functional space descriptions. Also looks at who should write the program and the roles of architects and consultants.

112. *Wisconsin Library Building Project Handbook,* by Raymond M. Holt. (Bulletin no. 8268) Madison: Wisconsin Department of Public Instruction, 1978.

> Overview of library facility programming and planning process. Topics covered include an overview of the planning process, needs assessment, evaluating alternatives, the building program statement, costs, site considerations, getting the project underway, architectural implementation and development, plans analysis, interior design and the selection of furniture and equipment, the construction phase, occupying the new building and evaluation. Includes sample sections of a program, suggested list of topics for a building program, suggested questions for use in interviewing architects, diagrams, tables, schematics, etc., and an extensive bibliography.

113. "Writing The Building Program: The Significance of AND," by Alderson Fry. *Bulletin of the Medical Library Association* 59.1(1971): 77-81.

Reviews basic requirements of writing a building program. Emphasizes the importance of understanding the interrelationships of functions, services, users and materials. Includes a brief bibliography.

1.1.3 Evaluation or Description of Actual Facilities

114. *Building Folders.* American Library Association: Chicago.

Unpublished set of files maintained at the Headquarters Library of the American Library Association in Chicago. All types of libraries are represented and each folder contains information on one existing library facility. The contents of the folders vary but they can include written descriptions of the building, photographs, slides, site plans and floor plans.

115. "Building Review 1982 and 1983," by D. Warwick Dunstan. *Australian Library Journal* 33(1984): 12-34.

Provides overview of library facility construction in Australia in 1980 and 1981. Includes data for state and public libraries, parliamentary libraries, university libraries, special libraries, education libraries and school libraries. Similar data and discussions for different time periods appear periodically in this journal.

116. *The Canadian School-Housed Public Library,* edited by L.J. Amey. (Dalhousie University Libraries and Dalhousie School of Library Service, Occasional Paper no. 24) Halifax: Dalhousie University, 1979.

Gives details, including facilities data, for numerous public libraries housed in school library buildings throughout Canada. Most reports include layout drawings of the library, and some include photographs and a bibliography.

117. "The Combined School/Public Library in Pennsylvania," by Lawrence L. Jaffe. Dissertation. University of Pittsburgh, 1982.

> Reports a study of dual purpose school and public libraries in Pennsylvania, including an evaluation of the facilities of these institutions. Includes a bibliography.

118. *Design and Planning: Libraries for Schools and Universities* by Friedemann Wild. New York: Van Nostrand Reinhold, 1972.

> Consists of photographs, plans, and descriptions of 38 public, academic and special libraries. Each entry gives data on the architect, architectural details, overall concepts, layouts, site plans, and elevations.

119. "Designed for Users," by Nolan Lushington. *Wilson Library Bulletin* 56.10(1982): 766-767.

> Provides evaluation guidelines to be used when visiting a library facility. Topics covered include signage, site location, parking, access for the physically disabled, space, functional areas, traffic flow, restrooms, acoustics, non-public areas, and mechanical, electrical and environmental control systems.

120. "Five Libraries Capture Architectural Awards," *American Libraries* 16(1985): 474-478.

> Describes the five libraries that received Awards of Excellence for for Library Architecture in the 11th Library Building Award Program sponsored by the American Institute of Architects and the American Library Association. The winning libraries are the addition to the University of Michigan Law Library, the addition to the Folger Shakespeare Library, the new Vail Public Library, and the renovations at the San Francisco University High School Library, and the New York University Graduate School of Business

Library. Includes photographs. Similar articles can be found periodically in this journal.

121. "Interior Planning For an Integrated Whole," by Marshall Brown. *Talking Buildings: A Practical Dialogue on Programming and Planning Library Buildings*, edited by Raymond M. Holt. Proceedings of a Building Workshop, Pasadena, California, October 3-4, 1985. Sacramento: California State Library, 1986.

Case study report of the interior design process at the Chula Vista Public Library and the Del E. Webb Memorial Library Addition at Loma Linda University Medical Center.

122. "Library Buildings in the 80s: Canada," by Michael Dewe. *Information Development* 3(1987): 114-17.

Reviews public, academic and national library construction in Canada during the early 1980s. Includes illustrations and a bibliography.

123. *Library Buildings, 1972 Issue,* edited by Herbert Ward and Sally Odd. London: The Library Association, 1973.

Provides brief descriptions of 26 recently completed public, academic and special libraries in Great Britain. Each entry includes site plans, photographs, and a narrative description.

124. "Library Designs Revisited: What Works - What Doesn't." *American Libraries* 18(1987): 1110-1116.

Three librarians briefly discuss their relatively new buildings, noting what has worked and what has not. The libraries included are Carleton College, South Regional/Broward Community College, and Avon Free Public. Includes photographs.

125. "Two Ways of Planning: Penrose and Chula Vista," by Morris Schertz and Raymond M. Holt. *Library Journal* 101(1976): 2456-2459.

> Contrasts two different approaches to facility planning. The process at the Chula Vista Public Library was based on complete and in-depth planning resulting in a straightforward construction phase, while the process followed for the Penrose Library at the University of Denver used a phased construction approach. Includes photographs and bibliographies.

1.1.4 Renovations and Additions

126. "Addition/Remodeling/Renovation," by Hoyt R. Galvin. *Library Space Planning: Issues and Approaches* (*LJ* Special Report no. 7, edited by Karl Nyren) New York: R.R. Bowker, 1976. 61-62.

> Checklist of points to consider when deciding whether to construct a new facility or remodel/renovate an existing one. Topics covered include site adequacy, space adequacy and flexibility, cost estimates and intangibles.

127. *Building a New Library or Renovating an Old: Some Things To Consider,* by Gerald B. McCabe. ERIC, 1980. ERIC ED 224486.

> Overview of the planning process, both for new and renovated facilities. Emphasis given to building exteriors, building approach and access, bicycle accommodations, lighting, fire sprinkler systems, carpeting, wall coverings, pest control and refuse disposal. The role of the librarian, the use of consultants and the use of library service statistics are also considered. Includes cost and capacity figures for two university libraries and a brief bibliography.

128. "Designing to Meet New Requirements of Differing Services," by Andrew S. Mathers. *Canadian Library Journal* 39(1982): 210-212.

Overview of problems associated with renovating library buildings built before 1960 in order to provide new services. Considers problems of meeting new building codes, new requirements brought on by changing user populations and attaining a positive cost/benefit project. Includes checklist of items to consider when judging the suitability of older buildings for upgrading and expansion.

129. "Do Our Library Buildings Have to be Discarded Every Fifteen Years?" by Elaine Cohen and Aaron Cohen. *Library Space Planning: Issues and Approaches* (*LJ* Special Report no. 1, edited by Karl Nyren) New York: R.R. Bowker, 1976. 56-60.

Discusses problems often associated with new library buildings, including inadequate and inappropriate staff space and the emphasis of facade over function. Also considers the idea that a new facility is not always the appropriate approach, given that renovating the original structure could solve many of the problems. Suggests that libraries conduct space inventories, and includes sample inventory checklists.

130. "Essential Decisions Needed in Planning for the Remodeling of Libraries," by R.H. Rohlf. *Catholic Library World* 51(1980): 280-282.

Reviews the major factors to consider when planning a library renovation project, including alternative approaches, the building program, physical condition of existing structure, space utilization and energy and regulatory code compliance.

131. "An Evaluative Comparison of the Satisfaction with the Utility of New Buildings versus Library Additions and

Addition/Renovations," by Gerald C. Sandy. Dissertation. Florida State University, 1981.

Reports a study comparing new library buildings with renovated facilities, based on the perceptions of library administrators and staff. Includes tables and a bibliography.

132. "Finding Space: Adaptive Reuse," by Phyllis Knapp Thomas. *Library Journal* 107(1982): 2230-2234.

Discusses the trend towards the conversion of non-library structures to library facilities. Describes decision process and the design and implementation of the conversion of three public libraries. Includes floor plans, facade drawings, and photographs.

133. "A Funny Thing Happened on the Way to the Addition," by George R. Parks. *Library Journal* 110.20(1985): 41-43.

Reviews the problems often associated with constructing additions to library buildings, including noise, dirt, water leaks, fire, "lost and found," temperature, humidity, errors in plans and pests. Includes a brief bibliography.

134. "Gaining Space by Creative Re-Arrangement of Library Areas," by Rolf Myller. *Library Space Planning: Issues and Approaches* (*LJ* Special Report no. 1, edited by Karl Nyren) New York: R.R. Bowker, 1976. 55.

Suggests using floor plans drawn to scale, together with cut-out scale drawings of current furniture, in order to find a better working layout.

135. "Hermit Crab Buildings," by Bud Oringdulph. *Talking Buildings: A Practical Dialogue on Programming and Planning Library Buildings*, edited by Raymond M. Holt. Proceedings of a Building Workshop, Pasadena, California, October 3-4,

1985. Sacramento: California State Library, 1986. 143-154.
ERIC ED 271109.

> Deals with buildings that were built for one purpose
> and are used for another. This paper is designed to
> accompany a slide presentation and the slides may be
> obtained from a source given in the article.

136. "Problems of Renovating an Existing Library Building,"
by Keyes Metcalf. *Running out of Space: What are the
Alternatives?*, edited by Gloria Novak. Papers from a
Preconference at the American Library Association Annual
Meeting, 1975. Chicago: American Library Association, 1978.
97-101.

> Writing from the point of view of a librarian, the
> author reviews 11 basic problems often associated with
> renovating an existing facility.

1.1.5 Legislation: All Types of Libraries

137. *Annual Report on LSCA Priorities, FY 1980.*
Washington: Office of Libraries and Learning Technologies,
1982. ERIC ED 219080.

> Summarizes information reported by state library
> administrative agencies for 1980. Includes reports of
> projects designed to provide services to the physically
> handicapped, the institutionalized, and the aged. Each
> area includes facility design considerations. Similar
> reports for other time periods can be accessed through
> ERIC.

138. *Annual Report on LSCA Special Activities, FY 1984.*
Washington: Office of Educational Research and Improvement,
1986. ERIC ED 269013.

> Contains six reports compiled by U.S. Department of

Education. "Public library construction, LSCA II," by
Nathan Cohen reviews the utilization of LSCA II funds
in FY 1985, a total of $24.5 million. Includes table
summarizing Title II construction, FY 1965-91985.
Similar reports on LSA and LSCA for other time
periods can be accessed on ERIC.

139. *An Evaluation of Title I of the Library Service and
Construction Act: Final Report,* by Joseph Casey, et al. Silver
Spring: Applied Management Sciences, 1981. ERIC ED
198823.

In-depth evaluation of the impact this legislation has
had on state-based efforts to improve and develop
public libraries. Includes history and background, study
methodology, uses of LSCA Title I funds, factors
affecting the use of LSCA Title I funds, changes in
library services and organization resulting from LSCA
Title I, effects on the coverage and accessibility of
public library services, problem areas and future
directions, and major findings and implications. Includes
extensive data analysis tables, appendices, and a
bibliography.

140. *Library Law and Legislation in the United States,* by
Alex Ladenson. (Scarecrow Library Administration Series no.
1) Metuchen: Scarecrow Press, 1982.

Overview of law and legislation related to U.S.
libraries. Topics covered include public library legislation
history, legal basis of public library organization, public
library governance, legal structure and function of state
library agencies, legal organization of public and
multitype library systems and networks, school libraries,
academic libraries and federal library legislation.
Includes a bibliography.

141. "LSA and LSCA, 1956-1973: A Legislative History," by
James W. Fry. *Library Trends* 24(1975): 7-26.

Reviews the historical development and application of
the Library Services Act of 1956 and the Library
Services and Construction Act of 1964. Includes a
bibliography.

142. *The Library Services and Construction Act: An Historical
Overview From the Viewpoint of Major Participants,* by
Edward G. Holley and Robert F. Schremser. Foundations in
Library and Information Science, vol. 18. Greenwich: JAI,
1983.

Based on a series of interviews with 13 major
participants in the LSCA, this book traces first 25
years of the LSCA. Topics covered include early
attempts at federal legislation for libraries, the Library
Services Act emerges (1950-19569), implementation of
LSA (1956-1960), battle for renewal of LSA (1960),
the Kennedy years (1961-1963), Lyndon Johnson and
the Great Society (1963-1968), and the Nixon years to
the present (1969-1981). Includes extensive bibliography,
chronology, and tables showing federal funds under
LSCA.

143. *Public Library Construction in 1965-1978: The Federal
Contribution Through the Library Services and Construction
Act,* by Ann M. Erteschik. Washington, D.C.: Bureau of
School Systems, 1978. ERIC ED 165813.

Summarizes state provided statistical data for federally
supported LSCA construction between 1965 and 1978.
Includes tables. Similar reports for other time periods
can be accessed through ERIC.

144. "Questions About LSCA Title II," by Cy Silver. *Talking
Buildings: A Practical Dialogue on Programming and Planning
Library Buildings,* edited by Raymond M. Holt. Proceedings of
a Building Workshop, Pasadena, California, October 3-4,
1985. Sacramento: California State Library, 1986. 109-112.
ERIC ED 271109.

Reviews some commonly asked questions regarding the Library Services and Construction Act Title II, Public Library Construction. Topics covered include who can apply, use of donated materials and labor, state involvement in design and construction, local matching funding requirements, renovations, furniture, funding sources, minimum project sizes, involvement of State Library, meeting deadlines, portable buildings, tips on gaining approval and further information.

1.2 Academic Libraries

1.2.1 Bibliographies, Standards, History and Multiple-Library Statistical Overviews

145. "Academic Libraries in 1876," by Edward G. Holley. *College and Research Libraries* 37(1976): 15-47.

Overview of academic libraries in 1876, including a discussion and photographs of several facilities. Includes an extensive bibliography.

146. "Academic Library Buildings: A Century in Review," by Jerrold Orne. *College and Research Libraries* 37(1976): 316-331.

Reviews academic library building development between 1876 and 1976. Includes photographs and a bibliography.

147. "Academic Library Building in 1970," by Jerrold Orne. *Library Journal* 95(1970): 4107-4112.

Fourth annual statistical survey of academic library building construction in 1970. In addition to basic statistics, it includes definitions of such terms as project cost, area, building cost, equipment cost, square foot

cost, and volume capacity. Includes list of academic
libraries built in 1970 and photographs. Similar articles
can be found periodically in the December 1 issues of
Library Journal.

148. "The American Academic Library Building, 1870-1890,"
by David Kaser. *Journal of Library History* 21.1(1986):
60-71.

Describes the changes in library buildings between 1870
and 1890 with particular emphasis on the development
of the dividing of space into three partitions to serve
users, books and staff. It concludes with an
examination of the limitations of the tripartition system
and how by 1890 it was being abandoned as libraries
were further divided into additional functional areas.
Includes illustrations and a bibliography.

149. "Architecture of Academic Libraries in Europe: A
Bibliography, 1960-1970," by Andrew Melnyk. *College and
University Libraries* 33(1972): 228-235.

Selective bibliography including both English and
non-English language entries.

150. "British Academic Library Buildings Since 1964: A
Comparative Study," by Anthony Vaughan. *Journal of
Librarianship* 12(1980): 179-198.

Reports a study of 53 large academic library buildings
in Great Britain. Comparative evaluation of the
buildings is made from the library staffs' perspectives
in regard to such factors as layout, functional
relationships, provisions for users and collections and
aesthetics. Includes tables, illustrations and a
bibliography.

151. "British Academic Library Planning 1966-1980," by
Harry Faulkner-Brown. *LIBER Bulletin* 16(1981): 32-38.

Proceedings of a Seminar held in Heidelberg in November, 1980 on library architecture.

Part of a special proceedings issue on library architecture, this article considers recent British library facilities from three perspectives, the thinking and philosophy behind the arrangement of ·libraries designed in this period, the external and governmental factors which have affected them, and the economic factors which will probably dictate the approach of future library design, with special emphasis on energy conservation. Includes a discussion of "Faulkner-Brown's Ten Commandments" for academic libraries: flexible, compact, accessible, extendible, varied, organized, comfortable, constant in environment, secure, and economic. Also includes tables, charts, and a bibliography.

152. "British University Library Buildings," by Edward B. Stanford. *Library Journal* 96(1971): 4067-4071.

Reviews the development of British library buildings 1961-1971. Discusses political factors, layouts, use of pre-fabricated materials, interior design, multipurpose buildings, closed stacks, compact storage, atria, elevators and stairs. Includes photographs and a bibliography.

153. *The Carnegie Corporation and the Development of American College Libraries, 1928-1941*, by Neil A. Radford. Chicago: American Library Association, 1984.

Detailed discussion of the relationship of the Carnegie Corporation and American college libraries between 1928 and 1941. Includes tables and a bibliography.

154. "College Library Buildings in Transition: A Study of 36 Libraries Built in 1967-68," by Michael S. Freeman. *College and Research Libraries* 43(1982): 478-480.

Analyzes 36 academic library buildings constructed

between 1967 and 1968 for such factors as storage space, seating space, building modifications, and other interior adjustments. Includes tables and a brief bibliography.

155. "The Curious Case of the Library Building," by Lawrence Lieberfeld. *College and Research Libraries* 44(1983): 77-282.

Reports study of how 37 academic library buildings are actually used in comparison with the building program. Analyzes the usefulness of various formulas, guidelines and standards used in planning, with particular emphasis on ACRL's "Formula C." Includes a brief bibliography.

156. "A Decade of Academic Law Library Construction 1967-76," by Roy M. Mersky. *Library Journal* 104(1979): 2519-2524.

Statistical analysis of law library construction between 1967 and 1976. Includes tables giving details on individual new and renovated libraries, as well as summary data on staff area sizes for various functional areas in the facility.

157. *Higher Education Planning: A Bibliographic Handbook,* edited by D. Kent Halstead. Washington: National Institute of Education, Department of Health Education and Welfare, 1979. ERIC ED 172621.

Annotated bibliography focusing on state and national higher education planning. Facilities related coverage includes campus and building planning, and space management and projections.

158. "Library History, University History, and Photographic History: Some Considerations for Research," by Boyd Childress. *Journal of Library History* 22.1(1987): 70-84.

Points out the value of institutional histories as sources
for photographs of library facilities which might
otherwise be very difficult to locate. Includes
illustrations and a bibliography.

159. *Planning Library Buildings: A Select Bibliography,*
compiled by George J. Snowball and Rosemary Thomson. 2nd
edition. Chicago: Library Administration and Management
Association, American Library Association, 1984.

Selective non-annotated bibliography covering the areas
of general works, architects and consultants, automation,
building program, costs and construction, environmental
control, floors, furniture and equipment, handicapped
access, interior decoration, media, moving, remodeling
and additions, signage, space planning, special
collections, storage and stacks, building reviews and
case studies, and bibliographies.

160. *Policies and Guidelines Developed for Community and
Technical College Libraries,* compiled by Frances
Davidson-Arnott. Ottawa: Canadian Library Association, 1983.

Reproduces the facilities related policies and guidelines
of four Canadian college libraries.

161. "Postwar University Library Buildings in West
Germany," Harold D. Jones. *College and Research Libraries*
36(1975): 283-294.

Discusses 20 West German academic library buildings
constructed since 1945. Includes photographs and a
bibliography.

162. "The Renaissance of Academic Library Building,
1967-1971," by Jerrold Orne. *Library Journal* 96(1971):
3947-3967.

Presents a statistical analysis of academic library

construction and renovation between 1967-1971. Topics covered include libraries over $5 million, libraries between $2-$5 million, undergraduate libraries, medical and law libraries, subject and division libraries, additions, additions plus renovation, multipurpose buildings and Canadian libraries. Article includes lists of building/renovation projects for each of these topics. Also includes photographs. Similar articles can be found in several subsequent December 1 issues of *Library Journal.*

163. "Science and Technology Academic Facility Construction in Louisiana, Oklahoma and Texas, 1977-1982," by Frank L. Turner, et al. *Science and Technology Libraries* 4.2(1983): 109-115.

Reports a study of 17 special academic science libraries, including the relevant funding and political factors.

164. "Standards and Guidelines Relating to Academic Libraries." *College and Research Libraries News* 45(1984): 474-479.

List of academic library standards published by the American Library Association and other professional organizations, several of which provide facilities standards. Includes Canadian guidelines and NISO standards.

165. "Standards for College Libraries, 1985." *College and Research Libraries News* 46(1985): 241-252.

Prepared by the Association of College and Research Libraries of the American Library Association. Standard no. 6 provides facility related standards, including formulas used to compute collection space requirements, user space requirements, and staff area requirements.

166. "Standards for University Libraries," edited by Beverly Lynch. *IFLA Journal* 13(1987): 120-125.

Contains the text of *The Statement of Standards for University Libraries* as formulated by IFLA. Includes Standard 6 which covers facilities.

167. "Standards for University Libraries in Pakistan," by Naimuddin Qureshi. Dissertation. University of Pittsburgh, 1982.

Reports on the development of a set of academic library standards. Includes details of the process, including how ACRL standards were used for comparison purposes. Includes tables and a bibliography.

168. "Twenty-Five Years of Academic Library Building Planning," by David Kaser. *College and Research Libraries* 45(1984): 268-281.

Reviews the development of modular building design and the changes made in the basic approach since 1960. Covers such problem areas as irregular shapes, interior and exterior courts, monumentality, and too much or too little glass. Discusses the relatively new approaches of high-rise and underground buildings. Includes photographs and a brief bibliography.

169. "Two-Year Academic Library Buildings," by Joleen Bock. *Library Journal* 96(1971): 3986-3989.

Provides five year statistical report on new two-year college library buildings. Includes junior colleges, community colleges, learning resource centers, instructional media centers and learning skills centers. Also includes photographs. Similar articles can be found in several subsequent December 1 issues of *Library Journal.*

170. *The University Library in the United States: Its Origins and Development,* by Arthur T. Hamlin. Philadelphia: University of Pennsylvania Press, 1981.

Within the context of a broad-based historical review, this book includes a consideration of the development of library buildings. Includes tables, illustrations and a bibliography.

171. "Wanted: Standards for Academic Law Libraries in Nigeria," by Christopher C. Ifebuzor. *Law Librarian* 18.3(1987): 81-86.

Within the general context of developing academic law library standards, this article contains a section on proposed facility and space standards. Includes a bibliography.

172. "The Yale University Library, 1865-1931 (Connecticut)," by Thomas F. O'Connor. Dissertation. Columbia University, 1984.

Detailed history of Yale University Library, including the planning of the Sterling Memorial Library building. Includes tables and bibliography. Several other dissertations and theses have been completed which detail the history of specific library facilities. These can be accessed through *Dissertation Abstracts.*

1.2.2 Planning a Facility: General Considerations

173. "Academic Library Building Planning and Design: An Overview," by Heather M. Edwards. *South African Journal of Library and Information Science* 55.1(1987): 16-21.

Based by the author on her MLS thesis, this article provides a general overview of basic planning and design principles and techniques for academic libraries.

Includes a bibliography.

174. *Academic Library Buildings: A Guide to Architectural Issues and Solutions,* by Ralph E. Ellsworth. Boulder: Colorado Associated University Press, 1973.

This book consists of pictures of over 125 academic libraries, with a total of approximately 1500 photographs. Several of the libraries are accompained by descriptions of their exteriors, interiors, and layout floor plans.

175. *The Administration of the College Library,* by Guy R. Lyle. 4th edition. New York: H.W. Wilson, 1974.

Includes chapter on the library building and equipment. Examines the issues involved in deciding whether to remodel/renovate or construct a new facility, the roles of the planning committee, librarian and architect, the library program, estimating space requirements for users, staff and the collection, and interior design and furnishings. Includes a bibliography.

176. "College Libraries in India," by M. Bavakutty. *International Library Review* 14.4(1982): 391-397.

Within the context of a general review of Indian academic libraries, this article looks at the physical facilities of these institutions. Includes a bibliography.

177. *The Community College Library,* by Fritz Veit. (Contributions in Librarianship and Information Science, no. 14) Westport: Greenwood Press, 1975.

The chapter on planning the library building provides a discussion of the building program, using examples from several existing facilities. Includes floor plans and a bibliography.

178. "Consulting on Academic Library Buildings," by Ellsworth Mason. *Library Trends* 28(1980): 363-380.

Provides overview of library building consulting. Discusses trends, deciding when a consultant is needed, how to select one, when the consultant should be hired, what the consultant does and the cost. Includes a bibliography.

179. "Converting Program to Costs and Cost to Funding Academic Libraries," by Nancy R. McAdams. *Talking Buildings: A Practical Dialogue on Programming and Planning Library Buildings*, edited by Raymond M. Holt. Proceedings of a Building Workshop, Pasadena, California, October 3-4, 1985. Sacramento: California State Library, 1986. 115-128. ERIC ED 271109.

Overview of costing process, including the topics converting net square feet to gross square feet of building for the basis of construction costs, determining the total project cost, sources of construction cost figures, cost estimating, sources of funding and cash flow.

180. *Cooperative Library Resource Sharing Among Universities Supporting Graduate Study in Alabama.* Montgomery: Alabama State Commission on Higher Education, 1982. ERIC ED 224497.

Includes report on determining space requirements, giving details on data collection methodology. Also demonstrates how two different formulas were used to determine space requirements, the Bareither formula and the Association of College and Research Libraries formula. Figures show library space in Alabama academic libraries and use of Bareither formula. Appendices give ACRL formulas and weighting.

181. "Cost Accounting and Analysis for University Libraries," by Ferdinand F. Leimkuhler and Michael D. Cooper. *College*

and Research Libraries 32(1971): 449-464.

Provides accounting models that can be used to
measure and evaluate library costs and aid in the
development of program budgets. Model includes facility
related cost analysis. Includes tables and a bibliography.

182. *Criteria for Planning the College and University Learning
Resources Center,* by Irving R. Merrill and Harold A. Drob.
Washington, D.C.: Association for Educational Communications
and Technology, 1977.

Contains chapter on criteria for staff and space in the
LRC. Topics covered include standards, criteria
development process and application of criteria. Includes
tables and a bibliography.

183. "Decision Making in Academic Library Building
Planning," by Joel G. Clemmer. *Planning Library Buildings:
From Decision to Design,* edited by Lester K. Smith. Papers
from a Preconference at the 1984 American Library
Association Annual Conference, Dallas, Texas. Chicago:
Library Administration and Management Association,
American Library Association, 1986. 69-70.

Briefly examines the relationships between the various
people involved in planning a library building and the
decision making process they can use to achieve
optimal results.

184. "Developments in the Planning of Main Library
Buildings," by Harry N. Peterson. *Library Trends* 20(1972):
693-713.

Detailed analysis of factors that must be considered
when planning library facilities. Emphasizes the need
for a well developed building program written by the
librarian.

185. "An Evaluative Comparison of the Satisfaction with the Utility of New Buildings Versus Library Additions and Addition/Renovations," by Gerald C. Sandy. Dissertation. Florida State University, 1981.

Reports a research study which investigated the opinions of academic library directors and department heads in regard to the overall utility of academic library buildings. The author found that there is a higher level of satisfaction with new rather than renovated facilities. Includes a bibliography.

186. "Factors in Space Planning for the Learning Resource Center," by Joleen D. Bock. *Library Space Planning: Issues and Approaches* (*LJ* Special Report no. 1, edited by Karl Nyren) New York: R.R. Bowker, 1976. 30-35.

Reviews guidelines and standards for space planning in two-year college learning resource centers, including specific data on nonprint, print, stock space, reader station space, and staff space.

187. "The Ideology of Flexibility: A Study of Recent British Academic Library Buildings," by Anthony Vaughan. *Journal of Librarianship* 11(1979): 277-293.

Discusses the impact of modular flexible design approaches on academic library design in Great Britain. Topics covered include fixed function vs. modular libraries, the ideology of the fixed function library, open access and the abandonment of supervision, the mixing of books and readers, flexibility and the learning resource center, the American experience, the inadequacy of the fixed function building, economic constraints and technical advances, and alternative approaches. Includes a bibliography.

188. "The Importance of Modular Planning in Academic Libraries in the U.S.," by Ralph E. Ellsworth. *Colloquium on University Buildings,* edited by K.W. Humphreys. (Special

issue of *LIBER Bulletin,* Supplement no. 1) 1972: 28-34.

Reviews the use of modular building design in U.S. libraries and the factors that led to their development. Discusses the advantages of the modular approach.

189. "The Initial Brief for an Academic Library and Its Development," by Harry Faulkner-Brown. *Colloquium on University Library Buildings,* edited by K.W. Humphreys. (Special issue *LIBER Bulletin,* Supplement no. 1) 1972: 13-21.

Reviews the purposes of the initial building program (brief), including three categories of factors which should be taken into consideration: policy, operational factors, and quality and design factors. Includes diagram of program design process.

190. "Involving Consultants in Library Change," by James D. Lockwood. *College and Research Libraries* 38(1977): 498-508.

Provides guidelines for deciding when a library needs a consultant, how to select one, and what a consultant does. Views the process from the overall perspective of the library rather than from a strict facility design standpoint. Includes decision model, outlines to use when working with a consultant and a bibliography.

191. "Library Building Trends and Their Meanings," by Jerrold Orne. *Library Journal* 102(1977): 2397-2401.

Reviews major forces and trends which may influence academic library building planning and design in the future, including both social/political and technology-based factors. Includes photographs and a bibliography.

192. *LSU: The Library Space Utilization Methodology,* by Richard B. Hall. (Occasional Paper no. 141) Urbana:

Graduate School of Library Science, University of Illinois, 1979.

Details a methodology for measuring the space utilization of academic library facilities. Includes a behavioral activity and occupancy analysis of the library and forecasts the potential impact of new electronic technologies on library facility planning. Includes floor plans, functional spatial relationships drawings and "head count" analyses. Also includes a bibliography.

193. *Mason on Library Buildings,* by Ellsworth Mason. Metuchen: Scarecrow Press, 1980.

Overview of planning library buildings. Part I discusses writing the program, lighting, air-handling systems and interior design. Chapters include extensive footnotes. Part II includes library building reviews for the following libraries, Beinecke at Yale, Rockefeller Library at Brown, the University of Toronto and the Sedgewick Undergraduate Library at the University of British Columbia. Each review includes photographs, floor plans and a discussion of the facility. Appendix I provides very brief evaluations for 105 libraries. Appendix II contains a model for a building program.

194. "Needs Assesssment for Academic Libraries," by Bob Carmack. *Planning Library Buildings: From Decision to Design,* edited by Lester K. Smith. Papers from a preconference held at the 1984 American Library Association Annual Conference, Dallas, Texas. Chicago: Library Administration and Management Association, American Library Association, 1986. 1-24.

Detailed look at the needs assessment process used to plan a new academic library or renovate an existing facility. Topics covered include the needs assessment team, the use of consultants, evaluating current and future space needs for people and multi-format collections, the expected lifespan of the building, the impact of new technology, projected changes in academic programs and a clear definition of the population to be served.

195. "Patterns, Processes of Growth, and the Projection of Library Size: A Critical Review of the Literature on Academic Library Growth," by Robert E. Molyneux. *Library and Information Science Research* 8(1986): 5-28.

Detailed overview of the literature of library growth patterns and associated models. Includes tables and a bibliography.

196. *Planning Academic and Research Library Buildings*, by Keyes D. Metcalf. 2nd edition by Philip D. Leighton and David C. Weber. Chicago: American Library Association, 1986.

Highly detailed consideration of the topic. Chapter topics include the planning process and library requirements, alternatives to a new building, planning preliminaries, the planning team and the architect, general programming, housing the collection, accommodating users and collections, space for staff and general purposes, budgeting and expense control, additions and renovations, master planning and siting, schematic considerations, design development and construction documents and concerns. Appendices include program examples, formulas and tables, equipment and environmental control for preservation. Includes tables, layouts, drawings, glossary, and a substantial annotated bibliography.

197. "Planning Library Buildings for Nigerian Libraries," by Ralph Nwafor. *International Library Review* 7(1975): 67-76.

Overview of Nigerian academic library facilities, including problems with present buildings, aesthetic vs. functional, organization and control, location problems, space requirements, fixed vs. flexible interiors and climatic factors.

198. *Planning Manual for Academic Library Buildings*, by Ralph E. Ellsworth. Metuchen: Scarecrow Press, 1973.

Overview and detailed guide to the planning process for academic library buildings, largely intended for those who are not experienced library planners. Topics covered include nature of planning, why planning sometimes fails, determining needs, conceiving and writing the program, selection of the architect, planning for growth, planning for electronic technologies, building costs, formulas and standards, physical requirements of entrances/exits, circulation, reserve, special collections, reader areas, storage areas, serials and office landscaping. Includes floor plans, photographs, functional spatial relationship drawings, standards, and a bibliography.

199. *Planning the Academic Library: Metcalf and Ellsworth at York*, by Keyes D. Metcalf and Ralph Ellsworth, edited by Harry F. Brown. Newcastle Upon Tyne: Oriel Press, 1971.

Discussion by the two authors on various aspects of planning, including accommodating user needs, space requirements and organization, modular approach, functional areas, mechanical systems, interior design and traffic flow.

200. "Planning the Library Building: Role of Librarian, Architect, and Consultant," by Rajwant Singh. *Indian Library Movement* 5(1978): 40-50.

Looks at the importance of a well formulated planning team when planning academic libraries. Also discusses involving students and the university governing body in the planning process. Includes a bibliography.

201. "Programming for the New Library: An Overview," by George S. Grossman. *Law Library Journal* 79(1987): 489-498.

Overview of the planning and programming process for

law library facilities, including preparing the initial program, planning for the future and space planning. Includes a bibliography.

202. "Recent Trends in West German University Library Building Planning," by Harold D. Jones. *College and Research Libraries* 42(1981): 461-469.

Reviews academic library buildings in West Germany in general and describes five libraries completed since 1973.

203. *The Smaller Academic Library: A Management Handbook*, edited by Gerald B. McCabe. Westport: Greenwood, 1988.

Intended for use in academic libraries serving populations between 200 and 7500, this collection includes an article on the planning and management of the physical plant. Includes a bibliography.

204. "Some Observations on Architectural Style, Size and Cost of Libraries," by Ralph E. Ellsworth. *Journal of Academic Librarianship* 1.5(1975): 16-19.

Discusses the relationship of academic library architectural design and the status of the library on campus. Also makes the point that questions of building costs should be considered not from a square-foot perspective, but rather in terms of how well the facility will meet future needs. Provides examples using several academic libraries.

205. "Some Thoughts on the Design of British Academic Library Buildings," by Harry Faulkner-Brown. *LIBER Bulletin* 25(1986): 40-52.

Reports on the ongoing research on and the implementation of facility design in the United Kingdom, with special emphasis on the importance of close relationships between the librarian, the architect, engineering consultants and surveyors. Also presents ten basic guidelines to be followed when planning an academic library building. Includes illustrations.

206. "Trends in Academic Library Facilities," by Nancy R. McAdams. *Library Trends* 36(1987): 287-298.

Part of a special issue on library buildings, this article examines recent and continuing trends in the planning and construction of academic libraries. These trends include differentiation of storage and user space, retention of existing facilities, incremental growth, tighter programming, increased protection of life and property, dispersal of special formats and equipment, and accommodation of nonlibrary functions. Includes a bibliography.

207. "Turning Needs Into Space Requirements: Academic Libraries," by Nancy R. McAdams. *Talking Buildings: A Practical Dialogue on Programming and Planning Library Buildings,* edited by Raymond M. Holt. Proceedings of a Building Workshop, Pasadena, California, October 3-4, 1985. Sacramento: California State Library, 1986. 41-44. ERIC ED 271109.

Outlines the process of translating a library's perception of a need for library space change into a numerical statement of needs. Topics covered include defining big picture needs, estimating space required, converting needs to numbers with space formulae, converting needs to numbers by deriving your own numbers, how not to do it, and what to do with numbers.

208. "The Undergraduate Library," by Jerrold Orne. *Library Journal* 95(1970): 2230-2233.

Describes the development of the separate undergraduate library concept. Includes consideration of the role of building design in the success of the library.

209. *University Library Buildings in Southeast Asia,* edited by
Peggy Wai-Chee Hochstadt. Proceedings of a Workshop held
in Singapore, 22-26 November 1976. Singapore: University of
Singapore Library, 1977.

Includes the printed abstracts of 19 papers dealing with
a variety of facility related topics. Accompanying
microfiche provide full text for the papers. Papers
include "Planning an academic library building," by
Barry L. Burton, "The Hong Kong Polytechnic Library,"
by Barry L. Burton, "University library buildings," by
Robin Gibson, "The University Sains Malaysia Library
Building," by Edward Lim Huck Tee, "Planning a new
library building for the University of Technology
Malaysia at Kuala Lampur," by Che Sham H.M.
Darus, "The University of Malaya Library," by Beda
Lim, "The planning of the library building at the
Universiti Pertanian Malaysia," by Syed Salim Agha,
"The University of the Phillipines main library
building," by Marina G. Dayrit, "Visayas State College
of Agriculture (VISCA) library building plans," by
Leonor Gregorio, "The proposed Silliman University
library building," by Girgonio D. Siega, "Chulalongkorn
University library," by Kind Tantavirat, "Kasetsart
University main library," by Daruna Somboonkun,
"Planning for the new Central Library, Khon Kaen
University," by Aphai Prakobpol, "Siriraj Library,
Mahidol University," by Uthai Dhutiyabhodhi, "The
planning and design of the new library at the
Singapore Polytechnic, Dover Road campus," by
Rosemary Yeap, "The Central Library, University of
Singapore, Kent Ridge," by Peggy Wai-Chee Hochstadt,
"Nanyang University Library," by Koh Thong Ngee,
"The Hasanuddin University library," by A. Rahman
Rahim, and "The proposed library building for the
Institut Teknologi Bandung," by Gordon Hazeldine. Also
includes a table of statistics for university library
buildings in Southeast Asia and bibliographies.

210. *University Science and Engineering Libraries*, 2nd. ed. by Ellis Mount. (Contributions in Librarianship and Information Science, no. 49) Westport: Greenwood Press, 1985.

Within broad context of academic science and technology libraries, this book contains a chapters on planning library facilities, and library furnishings and equipment. Topics covered in the planning chapter include preplanning, the planning team, the program, space requirements, layout, stack areas, staff areas, space for audiovisual and electronic equipment, and environmental control. Describes three existing facilities and includes floor plans. Provides guidelines on moving the library and includes a bibliography. Topics in furnishings chapter include stacks, tables and carrels, filing cabinets, floor coverings, color selection, and equipment, together with a bibliography.

211. "You Have No One to Blame But Yourself," by Lyndon Vivrette and James A. Clark. *Community and Junior College Libraries* 2.4(1984): 5-12.

Looks at the importance of implementing an organized and logical approach to planning a new or renovated library building prior to the selection of the architect, with emphasis on the responsibilities of the librarian during the process.

1.2.3 Evaluation or Description of Actual Facilities

212. "Abilene Christian: The Margaret and Herman Brown Library." *Library Journal* 95(1970): 4144.

Describes the architectural design and interior layout of Margaret and Herman Brown Library at Abilene Christian College. Includes photographs and building data. Similar brief facility descriptions can be found periodically in this journal.

213. *Academic Library Development Program: A Self-Study.*
Pittsburgh: University Libraries, Carnegie-Mellon University,
1978. ERIC ED 191492.

> Presents results of four-month self-study which utilized
> the Academic Library Development Program (ALDP).
> One of the four areas evaluated is technology and
> facilities. Includes consideration of space requirements,
> maintenance and furnishings, and equipment, together
> with recommendations for solutions to problems in these
> areas. Also includes appendices giving study
> methodology and results. Particular emphasis is given to
> periodical and microform considerations. Includes
> extensive data analysis tables and charts and a
> bibliography. Similar self-studies for other academic
> libraries can be accessed through ERIC.

214. *Academic Library Development Program: Report of the
Self-Study*, compiled by Ronald P. Naylor, et al. Washington:
Association of Research Libraries, 1983. ERIC ED 245678.

> Reports results of a self-study of the Otto G. Richter
> Library at the University of Miami using the Academic
> Library Development Program (ALDP). Included is a
> task force report on technology and facilities, a section
> of which presents space utilization and layout
> evaluations and recommendations. Floor plans, layouts,
> and space inventories are given. Includes the data
> collection instrument and an extensive bibliography.
> Other examples of this type of study can be accessed
> through ERIC.

215. "Aesthetics vs Function, or an (Almost) Ideal
Combination, by Heather Colbert. *Wits Journal of
Librarianship and Information Science* 2(1983): 3-14.

> Describes the planning and construction of the Biological
> and Physical Sciences Library at Witwatersrand
> University in South Africa. Includes illustrations and a
> bibliography.

216. *Annual Survey of Howard University: The Library System, Services, and Facilities.* Washington: Office of Education, 1971. ERIC ED 056737.

Report on the Howard University library system, including a seven page section on facilities. Includes description of Founders Library (central library), Engineering and Architecture Library, Chemistry Library, School of Religion Library, Fine Arts Reading Room, Social Work Library, College of Law Library, Medical-Dental Library, Pharmacy Library and Nursing Library. Five specific recommendations for the improvement of facilities are given.

217. "Anticipating Needs of Users," by Edward P. Miller. *The User Encounters the Library: An Interdisciplinary Focus on the User/System Interface,* edited by Martin B. Steffenson and Larry D. Larason. Proceedings of a Library Training Institute, Monroe, Louisiana, July 31-August 3, 1978. Monroe: Northeast Louisiana University, 1986. 1-22. ERIC ED 266791.

Reviews several elements of user/system interface in academic libraries, including the environmental and physical. Includes description of evaluation process designed to measure quantitatively the effectiveness of a library in meeting user needs. Has a brief bibliography and includes flowcharts of selected library processes.

218. "An Architect's Perspective," by Kenneth Rohfling. *Law Library Journal* 79(1987): 499-519.

Within the context of a general consideration of the architect selection process, this article looks at the planning and design of new law library facilities at the University of Michigan, the University of Iowa and Duke University. Includes illustrations.

219. *An Assessment of Learning Resource Services,* by James P. Platte and Mort Mattson. Lansing: Lansing Community

College, 1978. ERIC ED 181953.

Reports results of study comparing the attitudes of community college students on three curriculum-based Learning Resource Centers as opposed to one centralized facility. Survey reveals that students prefer the decentralized facility approach.

220. "Beneath the Halls of Ivy: Avery Library Extension, Columbia University, New York." *Progressive Architecture* 59.3(1978): 60-61.

Describes the design of an underground addition to a large academic library, including the addition of an auditorium and exhibit area. Includes photographs, elevation drawing, floor plan, and architectural and construction data.

221. "Building Study: Central Library, Portsmouth Polytechnic," by Paul Koralek, et al. *Architect's Journal* 169(1979): 683-699.

Presents three views of the same library building project, from the perspectives of the architect, a user, and an engineer.

222. *Colorado Academic Library Master Plan: Revised Edition,* edited by Claude Johns and Beverly Moore. Pueblo: University of Southern Colorado, 1985. ERIC ED 261690.

Evaluates the strengths and weaknesses of private and public academic libraries in Colorado and reviews the potential role of these libraries in support of higher education. Appendix G is concerned with library and media center facility design guidelines, including the factors of evaluation, study methodology, planning standards, stack space, reader space, service space, collection size criteria, library media center space planning and library building program requirements. Reviews the facility planning standards and guidelines of several states and the American Library Association. Provides shelving space equivalents for selected nonprint media. Similar long and short range plans can be accessed for other institutions through ERIC.

223-224. "The Decision to Build a New Central Library at the University of Texas at Austin," by Nancy R. McAdams. *Running Out of Space: What are the Alternatives?*, edited by Gloria Novak. Papers from a Preconference at the American Library Association Annual Meeting, 1975. Chicago: American Library Association, 1978. 107-118.

Reviews the process used to decide to construct a new main library rather than renovate the existing stack tower library. Includes tables.

225. *De Pauw University Libraries Self-Study Report*, by Larry L. Hardesty. Washington: Association of Research Libraries, 1982. ERIC ED 217862.

Presents series of recommendations for improvement of facilities and services in the library, including the creation of a library building program before any major changes are made in the facility. Appendix provides overview of library building program process, including planning committee membership, rationale for program and typical components of a program. Similar self-studies for other institutions can be accessed through ERIC.

226. "Evaluation of the Academic Library: Space Allocation," by J.L. Schofield and D.H. Waters. *Journal of Librarianship* 8(1976): 175-184.

Provides a practical technique that librarians can use to evaluate space in a library, including general guidelines, quantitative measures, effectiveness measures and developing a new layout. Includes tables and a bibliography.

227. "Facilities of Swarthmore College's Science and Engineering Library," by Michael J. Durkan and Emik Horikawa. *Science and Technology Libraries* 3.4(1983): 95-104.

Describes the planning and construction of a new academic science and engineering library, including how space requirements were established. Includes illustrations and a bibliography.

228. "Facilities of the Kresge Engineering Library at the University of California, Berkeley," by Patricia Davitt Maughan. *Science and Technology Libraries* 3.4(1983): 85-93.

Reports the history, planning, design, and architectural features of a new academic engineering library. Includes illustrations.

229. "The Failure of the Divisional Plan at Drake", by Thomas P. Slavens. *Library Space Planning: Issues and Approaches* (*LJ* Special Report no. 1, edited by Karl Nyren) New York: R.R. Bowker, 1976. 48-49.

Describes the divisional arrangement used at Drake University and explains why it failed, largely because of the unsuitability of the building, staff conflicts and budget problems.

230. "In Deference to Its Environment, The Pusey Library Was Built Beneath Harvard Yard." *Architectural Record* 160.4(1976): 97-102.

Describes design of underground academic library, including exterior design, site plans, layout plans and photographs.

231. "The John Crerar Library of the University of Chicago," by Patricia K. Swanson. *Science and Technology Libraries* 7.1(1986): 31-43.

Looks at the new facility designed to house the joint collections of the John Crerar Library and the University of Chicago. Discusses the new building and the move. Includes basic architectural and space usage statistics, a photograph, a layout drawing and a bibliography.

232. "Librarians as Interior Designers: The Icing on the Cake," by Dan Arnsan. *Community and Junior College Libraries* 3.3(1985): 21-32.

Reports the planning and implementation of the interior design of the LRC at Palomar College in California. The project was undertaken by the library staff and did not use the services of a consultant or interior designer. Includes illustrations.

233. "L.I.U. Library: A Final Campus Link." *Architectural Record* 160.1(1976): 93-98.

Describes the library at the Brooklyn Center branch of Long Island University and the role it plays in unifying a campus of buildings that were originally almost all constructed for other uses. Includes photographs and floor plans.

234. *New Academic Library Buildings*, edited by Karl Nyren. (*LJ* Special Report no. 16) New York: R.R. Bowker, 1980.

Presents brief descriptions of 16 recently completed or renovated academic libraries. Each library's description includes a statement by the Head Librarian, information on the architects and the architectural approach used, floor plans and photographs.

235. *New Academic Library Buildings II*, edited by Karl Nyren. (*LJ* Special Report no. 16) New York: R.R. Bowker, 1982.

Looks at 20 recently completed or renovated academic library buildings. Each library's description includes a statement by the Head Librarian, information on the architects and the architectural approach used, floor plans and photographs.

236. "New Concepts for Library Buildings: A Contribution from Sweden," by Thomas Tottie. *LIBER Bulletin* 25(1986): 53-56.

Looks at the planning of several academic library buildings in Sweden, discussing both new and renovated facilities.

237. "New Facility: Conservation Center Library, Institute of Fine Arts, New York University," by Evelyn K. Samuel. *Art Documentation* 1(1982): 112-113.

Brief review of the process involved in planning and constructing the Conservation Center Library, part of the overall renovation of a town house into the Conservation Center. Includes brief description of preliminary program, shelving, collection space requirements, floor layout design, and a variety of problems encountered during the process. Includes building section drawing showing location of the library and its relationship to other functional areas.

238. "The New Library Building at the University of Texas Health Science Center at San Antonio," by David A. Kronick, et al. *Bulletin of the Medical Library Association* 73(1985): 168-175.

Reports on the planning, construction, and move into a new special academic library building. Looks at the architectural features of the facility, layout and the special consideration given to new technology. Includes illustrations and a bibliography. This journal regularly reports on new medical libraries and similar articles can be accessed through *Library Literature* or *LISA*.

239. New Library Building: Mercer University School of Medicine, Macon, Georgia," by Joycelyn A. Rankin and George R. Bernard. *Bulletin of the Medical Library Association* 72(1984): 202-207.

Reports on the planning, design, and layout of a new academic medical library. Includes illustrations and a brief bibliography.

240. "New Library Buildings: The Health Sciences Library, Memorial University of Newfoundland, St. John's," by Richard B. Fredericksen. *Bulletin of the Medical Library Association* 67(1979): 313-321.

Looks at a new single level academic medical library, which was occupied using a phased occupancy approach. Examines the benefits and implications of single level facilities. Includes illustrations and a bibliography. See other issues of this journal for similar reports on other new or renovated facilities.

241. "New Library Buildings: The Houston Academy of Medicine-Texas Medical Center Library," by Samuel Hitt and Richard A. Lyders. *Bulletin of the Medical Library Association* 65(1977): 268-276.

Following a brief history of the library, this article looks in detail at the planning and design of the new facility and the renovation of the old library's interiors. Includes a table showing information on the architects, space capacities for users and collections, costs. Includes illustrations. See other issues of this journal for similar reports on other new or renovated facilities.

242. "On the Planning of a New Library," by Margaret Amosu. *Nigerian Libraries* 10(1974): 141-147.

Reports the planning, design, and construction of the library of the Medical School of the University of Ibadan in Nigeria.

243. "The Open Plan and Flexibility," by Harry
Faulkner-Brown. *IATUL Proceedings* 11(1979): 3-18.

Presents ten "commandments" for library planning and
design and looks at how these can be applied
successfully in an open plan building. Gives plans and
architectural design statistics for two academic libraries,
Cardiff and Notingham Universities. Includes
illustrations.

244. "Planning a New Library for Sydney Technical College,"
by Janet Goud. *Australasian College Libraries* 2(1984): 20-22.

Describes the programming process for a new academic
library building in Australia. Reviews the problems
involved in planning and the difficulties in applying
established standards.

245. "Planning, Timing, and Funding: Profile of the Santa
Monica College Library and Resource Center," by Letitia K.
Aaron, et al. *Community and Junior College Libraries*
2.4(1984): 13-23.

Looks at the planning, design and construction of a
new facility over an eight year period, during which
continued progress was threatened several times by
various political and funding factors. Includes
illustrations.

246. "Polytechnic Library, Portsmouth." *Architectural Review*
165(1979): 198-203.

Describes a polytechnic library designed like a
segmented pyramid covered by a concrete "tent."
Includes photographs, site plan, section drawings, floor
plans and architectural data.

247. "Ralph Pickard Bell Library, Mount Allison University,"
by Eleanor E. Magee. *Canadian Library Journal* 30(1973):

210-212.

Outlines the planning process used to design and build a small undergraduate library, including site selection, size and shape of the building, construction materials, interior design, flexibility and the importance of establishing good rapport with the architects.

248. "Rosary College: Staircase Surrounded by a Library." *Library Journal* 95(1970): 4142-4143.

Describes the architectural design and interior layout of Rosary College Library and Library Science Building in San Antonio, Texas. Includes photographs and building data.

249. "Sensation in San Diego." *Library Journal* 95(1970): 4145.

Looks at the architectural design and interior layout of the Central University Library, University of California at San Diego. Includes photographs and building data.

250. "The Spine or the Heart: The University of Jos in Search of a Library Building Model," by B.U. Nwafor. *College and Research Libraries* 42(1981): 447-455.

Discusses the proposed use of the spine library building concept at the University of Jos, Nigeria. Covers advantages and disadvantages of the approach and provides rationale for why the idea was ultimately rejected. Includes a bibliography.

251. "A Study of the Architectural Design of Six University Library Buildings," by Lester Kay Smith. Dissertation. University of Southern California, 1973.

Reports a study of six university library buildings erected between 1963-1973 which were designated as

being representative of "good" design. Based on
interviews and questionnaires sent to faculty, students,
and library staff, the following architectural
characteristics were judged the most controversial:
ventilation, noise control, number and location of
windows, library staff space and staff rest rooms.
Includes tables and a bibliography.

252. "...A Thing of Beauty," by Thomas Kabdebo. *An
Leabharlann, The Irish Library* 4.2(1987): 47-52.

Describes the new John Paul II Library at St.
Patrick's College, Ireland. Includes architectural
description and size and capacity descriptions. Also
includes tables and illustrations.

253. "Two College Libraries: One Designed to Occupy a City
Corner Site, the Other Shaped to Overlook a Campus
Green," by Mildred F. Schmertz. *Architectural Record* 8(1974):
97-108.

Contrasts the comparably sized Harvard Graduate
School of Education Library and the Bates College
Library, both of which use a multi-story open plan
design and were required to take the historic nature of
the surrounding neighborhoods into account. The Bates
Library planners used a much more systematic type of
planning approach than did the Harvard designers.
Includes photographs.

254. *The Undergraduate Library*, by Irene A. Braden. (ACRL
Monograph no. 31) Chicago: Association of College and
Research Libraries, American Library Association, 1970.

Presents detailed descriptions of six undergraduate
libraries, including Lamont Library at Harvard, Uris
Library at Cornell, and the undergraduate libraries at
Michigan, South Carolina, Indiana and Texas. Each
description includes a discussion of the physical facility
and interior design. Includes floor plans, photographs,

tables, and a bibliography.

255. "Underground Libraries," by Rolf Fuhlrott. *College and Research Libraries* 47(1986): 238-262.

Reviews advantages, disadvantages and design considerations involved in underground libraries, followed by detailed descriptions of major recently constructed underground libraries. Includes floor plans, site plans, photographs of the libraries and an extensive bibliography.

256. "Underneath the Oak Trees: The Sedgewick Undergraduate Library at U.B.C.," by Ellsworth Mason. *Journal of Academic Librarianship* 2(1977): 286-292.

Describes the strengths and weaknesses of this underground library at the University of British Columbia.

257. "Understatement: University of British Columbia, Vancouver." *Progressive Architecture* 54.3(1973): 86-91.

Describes design of underground academic library and the inclusion of five library-defined required environments for study. Includes elevation drawings, section drawings, site plan, floor plans, isometric drawing, photographs and architectural and construction data.

258. "University: Library Planning: The Experience of the University of Petroleum and Minerals," by M. Saleh Ashoor. *International Library Review* 15(1983): 273-289.

Overview of five-year plan for academic library in Saudi Arabia, including library space and facility factors and moving the library. Includes charts and tables.

259. "University of British Columbia: The Decision to Build an Underground Addition," by William Watson. *Running Out of Space: What are the Alternatives?*, edited by Gloria Novak. Papers from a Preconference at the American Library Association Annual Meeting, 1975. Chicago: American Library Association, 1978. 102-106.

> Describes a separate underground library facility, including the planning process, design features and evaluation. Includes a table giving basic building and architectural statistics.

260. "The University of Calabar Definitive Library Building: History and Future Development," by Lishi Kwasitsu. *Libri* 35(1985): 218-226.

> Looks at the planning of a new academic library building in Nigeria, including a discussion of the standards and specifications which were used. Includes illustrations and a bibliography.

261. "Use of the Delphi Technique: University Community Involvement in the Creation of a Library Building Program at Florida Institute of Technology," by Llewellyn L. Henson. Dissertation. Florida State University, 1980.

> Describes Delphi-based techniques used to generate data used in the preparation of an academic library building program. Includes tables and a bibliography.

262. "Without Grounds: The University of Winnipeg." *Progressive Architecture* 54.3(1973): 80-85.

> Describes a new building designed to provide a library, multimedia center, and teaching facilities, using a relatively small piece of land. Includes photographs, elevation drawings, floor plans and architectural and construction data.

1.2.4 Renovations and Additions

263. "The ABC's of Remodeling/Enlarging and Academic Library Building: A Personal Statement," by Ralph E. Ellsworth. *Journal of Academic Librarianship* 7(1982): 334-343.

Discusses the factors that probably will help determine the future size and design of academic library buildings. Includes remodeling checklist to indicate when renovation may not be appropriate, procedure for analyzing a library for remodeling and general comments on renovation. Includes "before" and "after" floor plans and descriptions of five renovated academic libraries and a bibliography.

264. "Building Conversions and Design Constraints," by Mary Cooper. *Library Review* 30(1981): 18-22.

Looks at the problems associated with the conversion of a non-library building into an academic library at the University of Strathclyde in Scotland.

265. *The Building of the South Wing of the Harold B. Lee Library: A Case Study in Library Planning and Decision Making,* by Anne Kathryn Grout. (Occasional Research Paper No. 3) Provo: Brigham Young University, School of Library and Information Science, 1982.

Describes the planning and construction of a extension wing on an academic library in Provo, Utah. Emphasis is given to the importance of flexibility in facility planning. Includes illustrations and a bibliography.

266. *Building Renovation in ARL Libraries: SPEC Kit 97,* edited by Rodney M. Hersberger. Washington: Association of Research Libraries, 1983.

Collection of reproduced documents from ARL libraries

dealing with facility renovation. Includes documents
covering such areas as storage, public service design
requirements, planning outlines and selection, program
and proposal requirements, planning outlines and
flowcharts. Includes layouts, tables, and a brief
bibliography. Several other volumes in the *SPEC Kit*
series are also at least partially concerned with facility
design and evaluation.

267. *Changes in Facilities and Services and Their Effect on
User Attitudes*, by Pat Weaver-Meyers and Jim Winters.
ERIC, 1984. ERIC ED 272218.

Reports results of a user attitude survey at the main
library at the University of Oklahoma before and after
the opening of a new wing. Areas studied include new
circulation services, new building facilities and collection
arrangement. Includes a brief bibliography and the
survey instrument.

268. "Getting From Here to There: Keeping an Academic
Library in Operation During Construction/Renovation," by T.
John Metz. *Advances in Library Administration and
Organization*, edited by Gerald B. McCabe and Bernard
Kreissman. 5(1986): 207-219.

Looks at the problems faced by academic library
administrators who must continue to provide services in
a building undergoing renovation. Provides detailed
outlines of a planning process and includes discussion of
preliminary steps, establishing relationships with all
involved parties, areas of concern, library requirements,
the library plan and implementing the plan. Includes
tables.

269. "Linking the Physical Past to the Program Future:
New Library Addition at the Medical College of Georgia," by
Thomas G. Basler, et al. *Bulletin of the Medical Library
Association* 71(1983): 386-390.

Reviews the planning process involved in designing and constructing an addition to an academic medical library, including the difficulties of linking the existing and new facilities. Also discusses the importance of integrating institutional and library goals when planning a new or renovated facility. Includes illustrations. Similar reviews of new or renovated facilities can be found periodically in this journal.

270. "Planning for Expansion at Wheaton," by Mark B. Mitchell. *Library Journal* 106(1981): 2290-2292.

Architect discusses the decision-making process used in remodeling the Wheaton College Library. Topics covered include centralization of branch libraries, non-centralization of audio visual services, creation of College Archives, collection growth projections, solicitation of outside funding for continuing facility-related costs, renovation vs. new building, space and architectural linkages with the rest of the campus, location of functions and departments in the renovated building and the restoration of an existing facade and atrium. Includes photographs.

271. "Remodeling and Expanding Space: Library Services During the Construction Period," by Anita K. Head. *Law Library Journal* 79(1987): 535-545.

Looks at the need for remodeling and expanding many current law library facilities rather than constructing new buildings. Examines the remodeling project at the Jacob Burns Law Library of George Washington University. Includes a bibliography.

272. "Remodeling Large Academic Libraries: Survival Hints," by Jane Conrow. *College and Research Libraries News* (1985): 600-604.

Discusses the renovation of the Hayden Library at Arizona State Library from the perspective of four

major issues, communication with staff and users,
signage, logistics and collection shifting. Includes "look
back from one year later" evaluation.

273. "Renovations in an Academic Library," by Sheila
Laidlaw. *Canadian Library Journal* 39(1982): 214-217.

Reviews the renovation process of the Sigmund Samuel
Library at the University of Toronto, including the
planning process, recognition of political climate and the
decision to keep the library open during renovation.

274. "Royal Agricultural College Library Extension," by M.J.
Long and Gordon Nelson. *Architects Journal* 24(1982): 56-68.

Reviews the planning and implementation of an
extension in Cirencester, England. Topics covered include
an interior design appraisal, energy system used and
cost data. Includes illustrations.

275. "A Wrap Around for the Quad." *Architectural Record*
173(1985): 106-107.

Describes the Lourdes Library Addition of
Gwynedd-Mercy College in Pennsylvania. The new
facility was wrapped around existing residential
buildings. Includes architectural details and photographs.

1.3 Public Libraries

1.3.1 Bibliographies, Standards, History and Multiple-Library Statistical Overviews

276. "An Alternative to Library Building Standards," by
Anders C. Dahlgren. *Illinois Libraries* 67(1985): 772-777.

Discusses the problems associated with the use of
established standards when planning a library building.
Describes the use of the Public Library Association's *A
Planning Process for Public Libraries* as an alternative
approach to broad based generalized guidelines. Also
considers the Wisconsin Division for Library Services' *A
Public Library Space Needs Outline*. Includes a
bibliography.

277. *The American Public Library: Research Report*, by
Donald J. Sager. Dublin: OCLC Online Computer Library
Center, 1982. ERIC ED 221222.

Broad based statistical analysis and overview of the
American public library in the 1970's. Five page
section deals with facilities. Includes consideration of the
relationship of size of population to the number of
libraries serving them, relationship of population size to
total square footage, relationship of population size to
seating capacity and relationship of population size to
hours of operation. Includes data analysis charts and a
bibliography.

278. "Benevolent Builder: Appraising Andrew Carnegie," by
Joseph Deitch. *Wilson Library Bulletin* 59(1984): 16-22.

Reviews role of Andrew Carnegie and the Carnegie
Corporation in the development of the American public
library and its facilities. Briefly covers the major
components of these buildings and the rationales
underlying their design. Includes photographs.

279. *Fact Book of the American Public Library*, compiled by
Herbert Goldhor. (Occasional Paper no. 150) Urbana:
Graduate School of Library Science, University of Illinois,
1981. ERIC ED 211054

Compilation of recent statistical data relevant to US
public libraries. None of the data predates 1970.
Includes several sections related to facility planning,

with bibliographic citations to the sources of the data in each entry.

280. "Heritage to Hi-Tech: Evolution of Image and Function of Canadian Public Library Buildings," by David R. Conn and Barry McCallum. *Readings in Canadian Library History*, edited by Peter F. McNally. Ottawa: Canadian Library Association, 1986. 123-149.

Historical development of urban public library buildings in Canada from 1899-1984. Includes photographs and a bibliography.

281. "H.T. Hare: Edwardian Library Architect," by Michael Dewe. *Library Review* 27(1978): 80-84.

Describes the accomplishments of H.T. Hare, an architect who designed nine public library buildings between 1897 and 1909 in the United Kingdom, using the open design approach, rather than separating different functions into different rooms. Includes a bibliography

282. "New Public Library Buildings in Ontario," by Grace Buller. *Ontario Library Review* 63(1979): 299-320.

Provides statistical data on 23 new public libraries built in Ontario since 1976. Topics covered by the data include architects, facility size, costs, collection capacity, user seating capacity, parking, handicapped provisions, population size served, staff and funding sources. Includes tables and illustrations.

283. "Public Library Building in 1970," by Hoyt Galvin and Barbara Asbury. *Library Journal* 95(1970): 4113-4134.

Statistical analysis and discussion of public library building construction and renovation in 1970. Includes list of new and remodeled facilities built in 1970, a three-year cost summary, a list of architects and photographs. Similar articles can be found each year in the December 1 issue of *Library Journal.*, although the authors vary.

284. *Public Library Buildings: Standards and Type Plans for Library Promises in Areas with Populations of Between 5,000 and 25,000,* edited by Sven Plougaard and translated by Oliver Stallybrass. London: The Library Association, 1971.

Traces the development and use of public library standards in Denmark. Topics covered include the basis for library facility standards, drawing up the standards, Danish standards, planning of library premises, and Danish building type plans. Includes space requirements, layouts, a diagram of the planning process and floor plans. Other countries outside the U.S. and Canada have also developed facility standards. These can be accessed through *Library and Information Science Abstracts.*

285. *Public Library Goals for Minnesota. Minnesota Libraries* 28(1987): 310-321.

Among the goals presented, one section deals with physical facilities. Topics covered include library size norms, site location, general building features, the exterior of buildings and the interior of buildings. Other states and governmental jurisdictions have adopted similar goals that can be accessed through such sources as ERIC and *Library Literature.*

286. "Space Requirements of Public Libraries," by Tuija Alanko. *Scandinavian Public Library Quarterly* 10.2(1977): 34-43.

Looks at the methods used by the Helsinki University of Technology to devise space standards and requirements for public libraries in Finland, giving the resulting standards. Includes illustrations.

287. *Standards for Libraries Within Regional Library Systems in Saskatchewan.* Regina, Saskatchewan: Saskatchewan Library Association, 1978. ERIC ED 169884.

Set of standards developed to support decentralized delivery of services and centralized technical services, including facility standards for small branches.

1.3.2 Planning a Facility: General Considerations

288. "Alternatives to the Central Library," by F. William Summers. *Public Libraries* 23(1984): 4-7.

Looks at the concept of a central public library facility and then considers several alternative design and siting approaches. Includes a brief bibliography.

289. "The Branch Library in the City: Options for the Future," *Library Journal* 102(1977): 161-173.

A "mini-symposium" on urban branch libraries made up of eight very brief papers. The topic of library buildings is touched on in each of the papers, including consideration of kiosks and porta-branches and mini-central libraries. Includes photographs.

290. *Building Libraries: Guidelines for the Planning and Design of Ontario Public Libraries.* Toronto: Ministry of Citizenship and Culture, 1986.

Manual developed to help librarians plan facilities designed to serve communities of 50,000 or less. Topics covered include the library building committee, selection and hiring of consultants, the planning process, the library building program, facility options study (feasibility study), siting, design and construction schedules, establishing a cost control system, schematic design, specifications, working drawings, contracts and funding sources. Appendices include sample interview questions to use when selecting an architect, sample library user questionnaire, sample checklist of case study facility evaluations and a site evaluation scoring scheme. Also includes tables, illustrations, and a bibliography.

291. "Designed for Users," by Nolan Lushington. *Wilson Library Bulletin* 57(1983): 848-849.

Looks at how appropriate use of architects can result in an innovative facility design. Discusses the approach taken by two firms that specialize in public library design in Connecticut. Includes illustrations.

292. *Designing a Medium-Sized Public Library.* (Library Information Series No. 11, Building Bulletin no. 60) London: Office of Arts and Libraries and Architects and Building Branch, Department of Education and Science, 1981.

Reviews the importance of good communication between librarians and architects in library planning.

293. "Developments in the Planning of Main Library Buildings," by Harry N. Peterson. *Library Trends* 20(1972): 693-741.

Reviews the concept, design and planning of main library buildings by analyzing the literature and relevant standards. Also reports the results of a survey of new or recently renovated main libraries in cities with a population of over 250,000. Includes appendices giving results of the survey and a bibliography.

294. "The Effect of Distance on Public Library Use: A Literature Survey," by Susan Palmer. *Library Research* 3(1981): 315-354.

In depth literature review of topic including, historical
perspective, current trends, distance and the library
user (mode of travel, elasticity of demand, shopping
patterns, community awareness, user characteristics,
library spacing, equity) and public facility location
theory (central place theory, distributed goods,
travelled-for goods, gravity models, elastic demand
models). Includes several tables and an extensive
bibliography.

295. "Entrance Area Strategy in Libraries," by Sven Hirn.
Scandinavian Public Library Quarterly 19.4(1986): 129-131.

Looks at the importance of correctly designing the
entrance areas in public libraries. Includes illustrations.

296. *Facilities Funding Finesse,* edited by Richard B. Hall.
Proceedings of the ALA 1980 New York Conference
Program, Financing and Promotion of Public Library
Facilities. Chicago: American Library Association, 1982.

Overview of public library facility funding processes and
problems. Individual papers include "Local sources," by
Richard L. Waters, "Private sources," by Kathryn
Stephanoff, "Public relations," by Frank J. Dempsey,
"State sources," by Fredrick J. Glazer and "Federal
sources," by Raymond M. Holt.

297. "Financing Public Library Buildings," by Richard B.
Hall. *Library Journal* 112.20(1987): 73-76.

Reviews and summarizes the various statistics on public
library buildings published annually in articles in *LJ*
since 1968. Discusses federal, state, local and private
sources of funding, as well as potential future trends.
Includes tables and a bibliography.

298. "Flow of Function in Libraries," by Nolan Lushington.
American Libraries 7(1976): 92-96.

Three short essays on the role of functional design in library facilities. Includes illustrations.

299. "How and Why the Urban Public Library Usually Winds Up in the Wrong Place," by Warwick Dunstan. *Australian Library Journal* 26(1977): 265-269.

Discusses the need to include library siting as a major factor in urban planning, giving examples using Australian libraries and providing suggested approaches. Includes a bibliography.

300. "The Information Center Library," by Nolan Lushington. *Library Space Planning: Issues and Approaches* (*LJ* Special Report no. 1, edited by Karl Nyren) New York: R.R. Bowker, 1976. 12-14.

Discusses the impact of public libraries serving as information centers. Looks at several areas of concern, including staffing patterns, easy access, in-service training, info-area design, building design, budgeting, the browsing library, the information library, present practice and the community served.

301. "Interior Landscape and the Public Library Building," by Michael Dewe. *Library Review* 30(1981): 4-12.

Overview of interior design and layout considerations in public libraries, with emphasis on European and British approaches. Includes staff office design, group spaces, shelving patterns and informal vs. formal interior design layouts. Also includes the floor layout plans of several Danish libraries.

302. "Library Architecture and Environmental Design: The Application of Selected Environmental Design Factors to the Planning of Public Library Facilities," by Julian L. Veatch, Jr. Dissertation. Florida State University, 1979.

Reports the results of a survey completed by 33 public library building consultants on the topics of doors, signage, windows and natural light, artificial light, acoustics, casual seating, study spaces, office environments, toilets and miscellaneous considerations. Each factor was rated on its usefulness to public library building planning. Includes a bibliography.

303. "The Library Building Program: Key to Success," by Lance C. Finney. *Public Libraries* 23.3(1984): 79-82.

Goes over the basic components of a library building program process for public libraries, including a discussion of overall purposes and goals. Also looks briefly at the recent history of public library architecture in the U.S. Includes annotated list of program components and a brief bibliography.

304. "The Library Building Tomorrow," by Richard L. Waters. *Library Trends* 36(1987): 455-473.

Part of a special issue on library buildings, this article presents an overview and discussion of factors which will potentially influence the planning and construction of future library buildings. Topics covered include the role of government, demographics, the service sector, the future information marketplace, staff and management concerns, education and training, technology, planning the building and the future library community. Includes a bibliography.

305. "Library Buildings: Form Follows Function?" by Thomas H. Ballard. *Library Journal* 110.20(1985): 44-46.

Considers the problems associated with "mini-libraries" and shared facilities for public libraries. Also looks at maximizing stack space. Includes a bibliography.

306. "Library Buildings in Denmark," by Sven Plougaard.

Library Interior Layout and Design, edited by Rolf Fuhlrott and Michael Dewe. Proceedings of the Seminar held in Frederilssadal, Denmark, June 16-20, 1980. (IFLA Publication 24) New York: K.G. Saur, 1982. 24-41.

>   Describes the historical development of public library buildings in Denmark since 1920, illustrated by floor plans from different periods. Discusses current building standards, model plans, flexibility, design principles, interior design and furniture. Includes floor plans, space requirements for functional areas and layouts.

307. "The Location and Siting of Public Libraries in Australian Capital Cities with Special Reference to Melbourne," by Douglas W. Dunstan. Dissertation. University of Adelaide, 1975.

>   Reports study of where 75 Australian public libraries are located and how their sites were selected. Includes tables and a bibliography.

308. "A Manual of Public Library Premise," by Sven-Olof Svensson. *Scandinavian Public Library Quarterly* 15.2-3(1982): 59-75.

>   Part of a special issue on planning public library buildings, this article presents a facility planning manual designed for use in Sweden.

309. "Minilibraries: When Bigger Isn't Better," by B. Franklin Hemphill. *Library Journal* 104(1979): 2517-2518.

>   Looks at the design and use of library facilities of 1500-3000 square feet, discussing changes in the minilibrary concept that have developed after several years experience with this type of facility. Includes photographs.

310. "Needs Assessment, the Point of Origin," by Raymond

M. Holt. *Planning Library Buildings: From Decision to Design*, edited by Lester K. Smith. Papers from a Preconference at the 1984 American Library Association Annual Conference, Dallas, Texas. Chicago: Library Administration and Management Association, American Library Association, 1986. 25-42.

> Written from the perspective of public libraries, this paper examines the use and importance of the needs assessment process in the successful planning and design of library facilities. Topics covered include analysis and projection of space requirements, appraising the existing facility, considering the alternatives of a new building vs. a renovated one and the "historic monument" syndrome.

311. "New Factor in Planning Public Library Buildings," by Robert H. Rohlf. *Public Libraries* 26.2(1987): 52-53.

> Looks at the problems and challenges associated with the calculation of facility and service plans based on non-local-resident populations.

312. "New Norwegian Guidelines for Public Library Buildings," by Aud Nordgarden and Rannveig E. Eidet. *Scandinavian Public Library Quarterly* 15.2-3(1982): 59-75.

> Part of a special issue on planning public library facilities, this article gives new building guidelines which take into account such factors as functional areas, siting, design and architecture, and compliance with regulations, laws and local conditions. Includes a table and illustrations.

313. "Output Measures and Library Space Planning," by Nolan Lushington. *Library Trends* 36(1987): 391-398.

> Part of a special issue on library buildings, this article traces the development of recent output measures for public libraries and discusses how they can be used in

conjunction with facilities planning. It looks at book capacity, frequency of use, technological developments and hierarchies of use. Includes a brief bibliography.

314. "Package Up Your Troubles: An Introduction to Package Libraries," by Colin Franks. *Assistant Librarian* 71.6(1978): 68-70.

Looks at the the basic concept of package libraries, a situation where the vendor provides both a manufactured building and all the furniture and equipment. Examines the advantages and disadvantages of this architectural and interior design approach. Includes illustrations.

315. "Planning and Policy," by Arthur Jones. *IFLA Journal* 4(1978): 103-106.

Points out the potentially serious problems facing public library facility designers in the near future. Includes such considerations as economic restraint and resource allocation in order to keep costs to a minimum while achieving maximum use of the facilities.

316. "The Planning of Public Libraries in Denmark," by Elisabeth Lylloff. *Library Interior Layout and Design*, edited by Rolf Fuhlrott and Michael Dewe. Proceedings of the Seminar held in Frederiksdal, Denmark, June 16-20, 1980. (IFLA Publication 24) New York: K.G. Saur, 1982. 42-50.

Discusses the programming process in Danish public libraries. Topics covered include analysis of requirements, schedule of requirements (space requirements), the brief (program), a case study example of how the process works and consulting activities. Includes a table of minimum space requirements for different functions and a sample schedule.

317. *Planning the Small Public Library Building*, by Anders Dahlgren. (Small Libraries Publication, no. 11, Library Administration and Management Association) Chicago: American Library Association, 1985.

> Provides brief overview of library facility process for small public libraries. Topics covered include the building planning team, space needs assessment and building standards, the building program, site selection, schematic design through construction documents, design considerations for the new library building, general planning notes, notes on functional areas (circulation, card catalog, readers, adult users, children, young adults, books, nonprint, workrooms, administrative offices, staff rooms, community meeting facilities, janitorial, restrooms, mechanical), other considerations (computers, energy efficiency, handicapped access) and alternatives to new construction. Includes bubble diagram, floor plan, site plan, guidelines for determining minimum space requirements, elevations, photographs, window and ventilation design drawings, and a bibliography.

318. "The Practicing Librarian: Public Library Parking Needs," by Hoyt Galvin. *Library Journal* 103(1978): 2310-2313.

> Based on a survey of new or renovated libraries, this article provides guidelines for the amount of parking spaces required by public libraries.

319. "Public Library Site Selection," by Robert H. Rohlf and David R. Smith. *Public Libraries* 24.2(1985): 47-49.

> Looks at the considerations that go into selecting the optimum site for a public library, including the shape and size of the site, cost and availability. Includes sample rating sheets and charts.

320. "A Public Library Site Symposium," *Library Space*

Planning: Issues and Approaches, (*LJ* Special Report no. 1, edited by Karl Nyren) New York: R.R. Bowker, 1976. 15-29.

Presents brief papers from a variety of authors on public library site selection. Topics covered include should libraries be in the business center, site planning in an urban, regional and communications planning context, site planning and service delivery, role of urban decay and renewal, trends in city development, core city siting, use of rented space, trends supporting Wheeler and decline of main branch use. Includes a branch site evaluation chart.

321. "Public Library Sites: An Informal Survey," by John Miniter. *Texas Libraries* 44(1983): 79-80.

Describes study of site location and selection factors for 72 Texas public libraries. Topics covered include nearness to "Main Street", use of consultants, purchase vs. donation of land, parking, and satisfaction with the site.

322. "The Selection of an Architect," by Robert H. Rohlf. *Public Libraries* 21.1(1982): 5-8.

Reviews the three major methods of selecting a library architect: direct, comparative and design competition. Considerable detail is provided for the comparative selection method, the most common approach, including a list of selection criteria.

323. "A Shared Housing Primer," by Mary L. Adams. *Library Journal* 111(1986): 65-66.

Overview of advantages and disadvantages of shared facilities for public libraries.

324. "Site Selection for Rural Public Libraries," by Virginia O. Schott. *Rural Libraries* 7.2(1987): 27-59.

Looks at the factors to be considered when selecting a
site for small-town public libraries. Topics covered
include the planning program, access, siting, building
size, building orientations, cost, parking, meeting local
zoning and code restrictions, matching the neighborhood
and town planning. Also examines the adaptive reuse
of existing facilities. Includes a bibliography.

325. *The Siting and Design of Public Library Buildings.*
Perth: Library Board of Western Australia, 1980.

Proposes procedures designed to result in an optimally
sited public library. Includes tables and a bibliography.

326. "Some Random Notes on Functional Design," by Nolan
Lushington. *American Libraries* 7(1976): 92-94.

Proposes that library architects and planners should
develop library designs that are functional and
immediately recognizable as community libraries.

327. "Space Planning for Community Information Services,"
by Robert Croneberger, Jr. and Carolyn Luck. *Library Space
Planning: Issues and Approaches (LJ* Special Report no. 1,
edited by Karl Nyren) New York: R.R. Bowker, 1976. 9-11.

Discusses the variables involved in space planning for
information and referral services, including type of
library, location, organizational structure, and the
information and referral model chosen. Considers space
planning for information processing separately from
space required to provide the information and referral
service.

328. "Spatial and Administrative Relationships in Large
Public Libraries: An Investigation into the Planning of
Municipal Libraries Serving Populations Exceeding One
Hundred Thousand," by Peter J. Bassnett. Dissertation. The
Library Association, 1971.

Reports a study looking at the relationships between types of management decision making and successful building and interior design approaches. Includes detailed consideration of various space allocation standards and formulas, functional relationships within the building, traffic patterns, housing the reader, environmental features and statistical data for the 45 participating libraries. Also includes numerous site plans, layouts, tables and a bibliography.

329. "Trends in Financing Public Library Buildings," by Richard B. Hall. *Library Trends* 36(1987): 423-453.

Part of a special issue on library buildings, this article briefly reviews the history of public library building funding. It continues with a discussion of funding sources, expenditures by category and future trends. Includes several tables, charts, and a bibliography.

330. "Trends in Public Library Buildings," by Raymond M. Holt. *Library Trends* 36(1987): 267-285.

Part of a special issue on library buildings, this article reviews recent and continuing trends in the planning and construction of public library facilities. Topics covered include financing, post-Carnegie design, siting, renovation, conversion of non-library facilities, building size, architecture, flexible space design, lighting, power, automation, telecommunications, fire and security protection systems, HVAC, energy conservation, work stations, interior design, signage and branches. Includes a bibliography.

331. "Turning Needs Into Space Requirements: The Public Library," by Raymond M. Holt. *Talking Buildings: A Practical Dialogue on Programming and Planning Library Buildings,* edited by Raymond M. Holt. Proceedings of a Building Workshop. Pasadena, California, October 3-4, 1985. Sacramento: California State Library, 1986. 45-63. ERIC ED 271109.

Reviews how a "Facility Needs Assessment," study can provide the information required for successful programming and facility planning, providing guidelines and formulas to calculate space requirements. Also discusses how a needs assessment can help develop goals and objectives, perspective and "nichemanship." The needs assessment process is outlined, including the collection, seating, staff, nonprint, evaluating the existing facility, the historic monument syndrome, alternatives and cost analysis. A chart provides a comparison of building project alternatives.

332. *Urban Analysis for Branch Library System Planning*, by Robert E. Coughlin, et al. (Contributions in Librarianship and Information Science, no. 1) Westport: Greenwood Publishing, 1972.

Detailed examination of how urban communities can be analyzed in order to provide optimal distribution of public library resources. Examines such facility related issues as site selection, capital value of the library, crowdedness, distance factors as related to use, effective service radius, layout, parking, seating space and availability of transit services. Includes tables, charts, index, and chapter level bibliographies.

333. *The Utility of Retail Site Selection for the Public Library* by William C. Robinson. (Occasional Paper no. 122) Urbana: Graduate School of Library Science, University of Illinois, 1976.

Discusses the use of retail site selection literature as a guide to effective library siting. Includes an extensive bibliography.

334. *Wheeler and Goldhor's Practical Administration of Public Libraries*, by Joseph L. Wheeler and Herbert Goldhor, revised by Carlton Rochell. Revised edition. New York: Harper and Row, 1981.

Includes chapter on facility planning, design and maintenance. Topics covered include the maintenance staff and their duties, lighting requirements for different functions, renovations and additions, the new facility planning process, use of consultants, building size, the building program statement, siting, interior design, plans, and staff areas and requirements. Includes tables and a bibliography.

1.3.3 Evaluation or Description of Actual Facilities

335. "Architect/Librarian Interface," by Harriet E. Bard and Jack E. Hodell. *The Library Scene* 6(1977): 4-6.

Reviews the different roles of the architect and the library staff in planning a public library. Uses the Morrisson-Reeves Library in Richmond, Indiana as a case study and includes photographs and tables.

336. *Beverly and Its Library: Report of a Self-Study of Beverly,* by Barbara Nelson, et al. Beverly: Beverly Public Library, 1976. ERIC ED 124192.

Self-study of the community and its public library, with a nine page chapter on facilities. Provides brief descriptions and evaluations of the main floor, the children's room, the adult browsing room, the stacks, the reference room, the youth room, the genealogy room, and the administrative and technical services areas. Floor plans are included.

337. "Building Study: The New Central Library at Wood Green." *Architects' Journal* 172(1980): 161-175.

Provides detailed discussion of new public library in England. Includes plans, photographs, and discussions of costs and energy requirements.

338. "Chestatee, Georgia: Library and Regional H.Q.,"
Library Journal 95(1970): 4139.

Describes the architectural design and interior layout of
the Chestatee Regional Library. Includes a photograph
and building data.

339. *Citizen Participation in Library Decision-Making: The
Toronto Experience,* edited by John Marshall. (Dalhousie
University, School of Library Service, no. 1) Metuchen:
Scarecrow Press, 1984.

Detailed review of the public library planning process
in Toronto and the role citizens played. Includes the
following facilities-related papers: "Branch library
renovation and citizen participation," by Alan Dudeck
and "Conflict, compromise, coordination: an architect's
view," by Jeffery Stinson. Also includes a photo essay
titled "The renovation process illustrated". The buildings
related appendices include a large bibliography, an
annotated bibliography of Toronto Public Library reports,
the "Five year objectives for the TPL, 1978-1983," and
the "Toronto Public Library Board capital projects:
policies and procedures, July 1978."

340. "A Community Living Room: Cleveland's Union Branch
Library," by Geraldine Kiefer. *Wilson Library Bulletin*
60(1985): 19-24.

Overview of new branch public library in Cleveland
which serves a largely minority patron group. After
reviewing the history of the branch, discusses the
planning of the new facility including site concerns,
type of facility required, and overall architectural
approach taken. Includes photographs and two item
bibliography.

341. "The Concept and Schematics Phase of Preparing
Architectural Drawings," by Richard L. Waters. *Planning
Library Buildings: From Decision to Design,* edited by Lester

K. Smith. Papers from a Preconference at the 1984 American Library Association Annual Conference, Dallas, Texas. Chicago: Library Administration and Management Association, American Library Association, 1986. 133-140.

Reports on the schematic design phase of the building project for the Dallas Central Library. Topics covered include the building program, selection of the architect, building shape, functional relationships, funding, furnishings, signage and maintenance.

342. "Consideration of Portable Structures in Meeting Library Needs," by Anne W. Paine. *Illinois Libraries* 67(1985): 813-815.

Describes the planning, construction and use of three modular portable branch public libraries in Fairfax County. Includes photographs and a floor plan.

343. "Cooperative Planning for a Successful Library Building," by Patricia McEnroe Koschik. *Library Journal* 111.20(1986): 67-69.

Reviews the planning and construction of the Meijer Branch library in Jackson, Michigan, which is located in a shopping center. Includes photographs.

344. "Design Today," by Andrea Michaels. *Wilson Library Bulletin* 61.9(1987): 40-44.

Looks at the new Birmingham Public and Jefferson County Free Library building in Alabama. Topics covered include site and structural elements, architecture, electrical, data communications, telephones, mechanical, fire protection, finishes, major functional areas (staff, group, children's, reference, etc.), special areas, signage, service points and displays. Includes photographs.

345. "Design Today," by Andrea Michaels. *Wilson Library Bulletin* 62.8(1988): 55-57.

Examines the design of the Michigan City Public Library in Indiana and San Juan Capistrano Public Library in California, both of which won design awards, and both of which the author judges to be unworkable facilities. Possible reasons for the failures are noted. This is followed by a brief discussion of several design elements which are important in achieving imaginative and functional buildings. These topics include ceilings, floors, walls, lighting, furniture, color, plants and signage. Includes photographs.

346. "Designed for Users," by Nolan Lushington. *Wilson Library Bulletin* 58.3(1983): 204-205.

Examines the Cockeysville branch of the Baltimore County Library System, which uses a special type of shelving that allows display of all the front covers of the books. Also discusses the design of the children's areas and special study and group meeting rooms.

347. "Designed for Users," by Nolan Lushington. *Wilson Library Bulletin* 58.4(1983): 284-285.

Describes the award winning Thousand Oaks Public Library in California, including a discussion of lighting, central reference, children's area, group usage rooms, parking, staff technical service areas and a special audiovisual area. Includes illustrations.

348. Does This Building Work?" by Edwin S. Clay and Gailyn Hlavka. *Library Administration and Management* 1(1987): 105-106.

Describes the development and intended use of a facility evaluation process for the Fairfax County Public Library System in Virginia. Questionnaires will be completed by both patrons and staff. Observational research techniques will also be employed, as will light and temperature checks. Includes a list of the topics included on the patron questionnaire.

349. "Dynamic Dallas: A Buildings Critique," by Raymond M. Holt. *Public Library Quarterly* 4.4(1983): 67-84.

Presents a critique of a large new public library building of over 650,000 square feet with space for a collection of 2,250,000 items. Looks at how the planning process was carried out, including the active participation of library staff. Includes illustrations.

350. "Happy Mall Fellows." *American Libraries* 16(1985): 154.

Describes a public library kiosk branch in a shopping mall.

351. *Henry County and the Public Library: Report of a Self-Study by the Blue Ridge Regional Library,* by Betty M. Ragsdale, et al. ERIC 1977. ED 165 734.

Reports results of an in-depth self-study of the library. Among the topics covered are long and short term facility related recommendations. Includes tables, maps and a bibliography. Similar reports for other libraries can be accessed through ERIC.

352. *The Hollins Branch Library and Its Community: An Analysis of Available Data,* by Frederick Roberts Reenstjerna. Roanoke, VA: Roanoke County Public Libraries, 1978. ERIC ED 161439.

Reports the results of a community analysis of a public library branch undertaken in order to develop short and long term goals and objectives. Part III reports facilities related recommendations. Similar reports for other public libraries can be accessed through ERIC.

353. "Instant Libraries," by Frederick Glazer. *Library Journal* 97(1972): 3874-3875.

Describes the "instant library" program of the West Virginia Library Commission using eight-sided glass and wood 1200 square foot buildings. Includes elevation and floor plan.

354. "Instant Library: 21 Days From Start to Finish." *Appalachia* 7.5(1974): 39-43.

Describes the "Instant Library Program" of West Virginia, including design details of the low-cost octagonal buildings, layout, floor plan, cost and a series of photographs showing construction.

355. "Library Architecture: The Cleveland Experience," by Ervin Gaines, et al. *Wilson Library Bulletin* 56(1982): 590-595.

Describes the philosophical background, planning, design and construction of a library Cleveland. Special attention is given to the role of the public and the place of the public library in an urban setting. Includes photographs.

356. "The Library Space Utilization Methodology," by Richard B. Hall. *Library Journal* 103(1978): 2379-2383.

Details the application of a model designed to yield optimal space utilization in libraries. It is applied to the Lincoln Library of Springfield, Illinois. Includes tables, diagrams, floor plans and a bibliography.

357. "A Library That Has Everything," by Geraldine W. Kiefer. *Library Journal* 109(1984): 2221-2223.

Reviews the planning and construction of a branch public library designed to serve a community of 10,000.

Includes photographs and a floor plan.

358. "Louisville: A Library Turnabout." *Library Journal*
95(1970): 4138.

Describes the architectural design and interior layout of
the North Building addition of the Louisville Public
Library. Includes a photograph and building data.

359. "Main Libraries: Time for Mutation?" by John F.
Anderson. *Library Space Planning: Issues and Approaches (LJ*
Special Report no. 1, edited by Karl Nyren) New York: R.R.
Bowker, 1976. 5-6.

Looks at the initial planning process for a new central
public library in Tuscon, Arizona. Emphasizes
consultation with non-library personnel during planning,
with particular attention to the areas of collection
organization, materials integration, technology utilization,
information transfer, the individual learner, community
development impact, and ecology and energy.

360. "The New Building After Five Years: an Evaluation,"
by Albert C. Lake. *California Librarian* 31(1970): 7-12.

Evaluates the Riverside Public Library based on five
years experience. Includes survey questionnaire.

361. "A New Central Library," by J.E.D. Stringleman.
Singapore Libraries 13(1983): 15-17.

Looks at a new library building in Christchurch, New
Zealand, including siting, planning and design,
construction and the move. Includes a table and
illustrations.

362. *New Public Library Buildings,* edited by Karl Nyren.
(*LJ* Special Report no. 8) New York: R.R. Bowker, 1979.

Provides descriptions of 19 new and remodeled public library buildings, including evaluative statements by the architects, library directors and library boards on the projects. Includes tables and illustrations.

363. *New Public Library Buildings II,* edited by Barbara Livingston. (*LJ* Special Report no. 17) New York: R.R. Bowker, 1980.

Descriptions of 18 new and remodeled public libraries, plus brief descriptions of several more. Each full description provides information on the architects and a statement by the library director on the facility. Photographs and tables providing basic facilities related statistical data on each library are also included.

364. *New Public Library Buildings III,* edited by Karl Nyren. (*LJ* Special Report no. 25) New York: R.R Bowker, 1983.

Gives descriptions of 19 new or recently renovated public library buildings. Each report provides information on the architects and a statement by the library director of the facility. Photographs and tables providing basic facilities related statistical data on each library are also included.

365. *The New York Public Library: Its Architecture and Decoration,* by Henry H. Reed. New York: Norton, 1986.

Reviews the planning and construction of the New York Public Library, together with detailed descriptions of the interior decorations and furnishings. Includes numerous photographs and a bibliography.

366. "On Time and Under Budget: Dallas Builds a Library," by Gail Tomlinson. *Wilson Library Bulletin* 56(1982): 217-222.

Overview of planning and construction of the large new Dallas Public Library. Includes photographs.

367. "Public Libraries." *Library Journal* 96(1971): 3981-3985.

Provides building data and photographs for ten public libraries constructed in 1970-1971. Libraries included are the Central Florida Regional Library (Florida), Shelter Rock Public (New York), Wantagh Public (New York), Lawson McGhee (Tennessee), Clark County (Nevada), Nicholson Memorial (Texas), Nokomis Branch (Minnesota), William Jeanes Memorial (Pennsylvania), Burlington County (New Jersey), and Southampton Free (Pennsylvania). Similar articles can be found most years in the December 1 issue of *Library Journal*.

368. *Public Library Buildings, 1975-1983*, edited by K.C. Harrison. London: Library Services, 1987.

Gives basic data on 581 public library facilities built in the United Kingdom between 1975 and 1983. For 100 of the buildings longer entries are provided which include brief narrative descriptions, statistics, floor plans and photographs.

369. "Putting Together the Planning Team - Case Study of Architect Selection Process in Redwood City," by Jane E. Light. *Talking Buildings: A Practical Dialogue on Programming and Planning Library Buildings*, edited by Raymond M. Holt. Proceedings of a Building Workshop, Pasadena, California, October 3-4, 1985. Sacramento: California State Library, 1986. 19-22. ERIC ED 271109.

Details the process used to select an architect for the Redwood City, California Public Library, including a discussion of City Council participation. Figure shows "Architect Selection Rating Sheet."

370. "The Second Generation Store Front Library," by B. F. Hemphill. *Library Space Planning: Issues and Approaches*, (*LJ* Special Report no. 1, edited by Karl Nyren) New York: R.R. Bowker, 1976. 7-8.

Discusses Baltimore County's book centers (store front libraries), a semiportable library building program. Describes the prefab, eight-sided, peaked roof structure of about 1260 square feet.

371. *Some Considerations for the Planning of Village Libraries in Tanzania, Occasional Paper no. 33,* by A.Z. Mwasha. Dar es Salaam, Tanzania: Tanzania Library Service, 1976. ERIC ED 220084.

Describes the planning of small village libraries in Tanzania, including recommendations for physical facilities. Includes a bibliography.

372. "Trouble in Second City," by Milo Nelson. *Wilson Library Bulletin* 62.5(1987): 17-21.

Reviews the history of selecting a site for the new main library building in Chicago, including an analysis of the management, political and financial factors which have contributed to major problems in the planning process. Includes photographs.

373. "User Evaluation of Three Branch Libraries," by Michael Durkan and Robert Sommer. *California Librarian* 33(1972): 114-123.

Reports survey research study evaluating user behavior and satisfaction with three public library branches. Provides data analyses for such variables as lighting, temperature, ventilation, room size, color, windows, furniture arrangement, comfort, noise, privacy, etc.

374. *The Yukon-Kuskokwim Village Library Project: An Evaluative Study,* by Edward Tennant and Audrey Kolb. Bellevue: Educational Research Associates, 1984. ERIC ED 262790.

Study carried out by Kuskokwim Community College of

16 village libraries in Alaska. Chapter on physical facilities emphasizes the importance of library site location, both in terms of location in village and as part of multipurpose buildings. Also evaluates such factors as size, furnishings, decor, shelving and equipment. Predictors of success related to the physical facility are provided, together with five specific recommendations.

1.3.4 Renovations and Additions

375. "Alternatives to New Public Library Buildings," by Barry Pettman. *Assistant Librarian* 71(1978): 65-67.

Part of a special issue on library building renovation and expansion, this article looks at renovation approaches in which the exterior of the building is retained, but the interior is completely renovated. Also looks at converting non-library buildings into library facilities. Includes illustrations.

376. "Alternatives to the Construction of a New Library," by B. Franklin Hemphill. *Library Trends* 36(1987): 399-409.

Part of a special issue on library buildings, this article reviews the various facility design approaches that can be used instead of a new building. These include rearrangements, additions, and prefab and portable buildings.

377. "Architectural Conservation and the Public Library," by David Arbogast. *Show-Me Libraries* 37.12(1986): 20-25.

Reviews the development of public library architecture in the U.S. Discusses the problems which buildings constructed in the last 30 years have developed, and contrasts this with the continuing value of older buildings which can be effectively renovated. Includes illustrations.

378. *An Architectural Strategy for Change: Remodeling and Expanding for Contemporary Public Library Needs*, edited by Raymond M. Holt. Proceedings of the Library Architecture Preconference Institute held at New York, New York, 4-6 July 1974, sponsored by the Library Administration Division, American Library Association. Chicago: American Library Association, 1976.

Provides case studies of eight recently remodeled or expanded public library facilities. Includes photographs, site plans, floor plans, and building data sheets.

379. "Branch Library Renovation and Citizen Participation," by Alan Dudeck. *International Library Review* 12.1(1980): 83-94.

Describes the process used by the Toronto Public Library to involve citizens in the planning of renovated library facilities by appointing members of the public to Branch Building Committees.

380. "A Critique of the Ferguson Library Stamford, Connecticut," by Aaron Cohen and Elaine Cohen. *Public Library Quarterly* 4.3(1983): 23-36.

Analyzes and evaluates the renovation and construction of an addition to a public library. Includes illustrations.

381. "Designed for Users," by Nolan Lushington. *Wilson Library Bulletin* 57(1982): 324-327.

Describes the renovation of the Ferguson Library in Stamford, Connecticut. The architects were required to double the building size with two additions while maintaining an existing Georgian-style facade. Discusses and evaluates how this was done. Article also describes the Aurora Public Library in Colorado.

382. "The Effect of Re-Siting a Library," by Arthur Jones
and M. Barry King. *Journal of Librarianship* 11(1979):
215-231.

Reports the changes in usage following the move of a
public library in England, including tables giving data
analyses.

383. "Finding Space: Adaptive Reuse," by Phyllis Knapp
Thomas. *Library Journal* 107(1982): 2230-2234.

Describes how a supermarket, a Victorian residence,
and a bank were adapted for use as libraries. Includes
site selection considerations, the importance of the
architect and an understanding of how the library will
be used. Also includes illustrations and floor plans.

384. "From a Sow's Ear: New Libraries from Old
Buildings," by Carol Steer. *Manitoba Library Association
Bulletin* 12.2(1982): 23-25.

Looks at the advantages of converting non-library
structures into library buildings and gives several
examples. Includes a bibliography.

385. "From Railway Hotel to Library," by Gustav Lundblad.
Scandinavian Public Library Quarterly 13.3(1980): 80-82.

Describes the renovation of a railway hotel into a
central main library in Storuman, Sweden. Includes
photographs.

386. "The Getty Square Library of Yonkers Public Library:
Department Store to Public Library," by Nolan Lushington.
Public Library Quarterly 6.4(1985/1986): 43-48.

Describes the process used to convert a department store into a public library. Includes illustrations.

387. "The Johannesburg Sun Hotel Public Library," by Denise Levin. *Wits Journal of Librarianship and Information Science* 4(1986): 33-53.

Reports the renovation of part of a hotel complex into a public library. Includes illustrations and a bibliography.

388. "A Library for the Future," by Mark B. Mitchell. *Library Journal* 109(1984): 2219-2220.

Reviews the conversion of several schools into public libraries. Includes photographs.

389. "Main Public Library Building Cincinnati and Hamilton County: A Critique," by Robert H. Rohlf. *Public Library Quarterly* 5.3(1984): 17-28.

Discusses and critiques a library addition opened in 1982, a renovation of an existing 1955 facility. Includes the directions given to the architect by the library and criteria established by the architect for the project. Describes the major components and features of the renovated structure.

390. "Planning Expanded Facilities: Issues for Small Public Libraries," by Anders C. Dahlgren. *Library Administration and Management* 1(1987): 80-84.

Reviews renovation planning factors of special concern to small libraries. Looks at identifying a realistic service population, problems presented by Carnegie buildings and other historic monuments, converting existing structures, plan for automation, shelving and seating requirements, and the use of common sense. Includes an illustration.

391. "The Public Library of Solvesborg and Comments," by Jan Lageras and Folke Frommert. *Scandinavian Public Library Quarterly* 18(1985): 74-76.

The librarian and the architect describe the adaptive renovation of a trading house into a public library. Includes illustrations.

392. "Recycling Isn't Just for Beer Cans," by Michael Dewe. *Assistant Librarian* 71.6(1978): 62-64.

Part of a special issue on library building renovation and conversion, this article looks at the trend towards renovation and expansion of existing library facilities rather than the construction of new buildings. It gives guidelines for a decision process used to determine whether to renovate, convert non-library facilities or undertake a new building. Also looks at the use of "package libraries", where prefabricated buildings are used. Includes a bibliography.

393. "Reutilizing Existing Library Space," by Marlys Cresap Davis. *Library Trends* 36(1987): 411-421.

Part of a special issue on library buildings, this article describes a planning process that can be used when renovating an existing library. Contains several examples using actual libraries. Includes floor plans.

394. "Special Report: From Service Station to Branch Library," by Otto Kramer. *Wilson Library Bulletin* 56(1982): 678-679.

Describes the renovation of a gas service station to a functional public library branch. Discusses the advantages of such an approach.

395. "Two Shropshire Libraries," by Roy Field. *Service Point* 29(1984): 4-9.

Describes the renovation and conversion of 16th century Riggs Hall and Castle Gates in Shrewsbury, England, into the Castle Gate Library. Includes photographs.

1.4 School Libraries and Children's Facilities in Public Libraries

1.4.1 Bibliographies, Standards, History and Multiple-Library Statistical Overviews

396. "Applying the T Square Between Program and Facilities," by Estella E. Reed. *Media Center Facilities Planning,* compiled and edited by Jane A. Hannigan and Glenn E. Estes. Chicago: American Library Association, 1978. 47-49.

Evaluates the facilities related standards and guidelines in the *Media Programs: District and School,* issued by the AASL and ALA. Topics covered include need for space, who initiates planning?, and agents of change. Includes bibliography.

397. "Facilities." *Media Programs: District and School.* (American Association of School Librarians and Association for Educational Communications and Technology) Chicago: American Library Association, 1975. 87-104. Reprinted in *Media Center Facilities Design,* compiled and edited by Jane A. Hannigan and Glenn E. Estes. Chicago: American Library Association, 1978. 41-47.

Provides detailed standards and guidelines for school media center facilities. Includes guiding principles, district program facilities, school program facilities, requirements of different functional areas, equipment and furniture and spatial and functional relationships. Includes tables and lists of evaluative questions.

398. *Indicators of Quality for School/Media Programs: District and School.* Chicago: American Library Association, 1979. ERIC ED 198797.

This study examines facilities design within the context of a multiple facility assessment process.

399. "A Review of Selected Doctoral Dissertations about School Library Media Programs and Resources, January 1972-December 1980," by Shirley L. Aaron. *School Library Media Quarterly* 10(1982): 210-240.

Evaluative review of recent research, including dissertations concerned in whole or in part with media center facilities. Includes an extensive bibliography.

400. "School Media Standards," by Jane Anne Hannigan. *Library Trends* 31(1982): 49-63.

Considers facilities related standards for school media centers, as well as non-facility standards. Includes a bibliography.

401. *Standards for Youth Services in Public Libraries of New York State,* by Julia Cummins, et al. New York: New York Library Association, 1984. ERIC ED 261699.

Includes very brief sections on facility standards for children's and youth areas, including handicapped access, furniture size and suitability, shelving requirements for both print and nonprint materials, displays, signs, seating, electrical requirements and environmental control.

402. *Statistics of Public School Libraries/Media Centers, Fall 1978,* by Robert A. Heintze and Lance Hodes. Washington, D.C.: National Center for Educational Statistics, 1981. ERIC ED 212297.

Based on a nationwide survey of 3500 public school libraries and media centers, this report contains data on space allocation and shelving in these facilities. Similar studies for other schools, types of libraries and time periods can be accessed through ERIC.

1.4.2 Planning a Facility: General Considerations

403. "After the Architect's Gone for His Reward," by Peggy Sullivan. *Media Center Facilities Design*, compiled and edited by Jane A. Hannigan and Glenn E. Estes. Chicago: American Library Association, 1978. 103-105.

Looks at some of the problems that can occur when a architect does not design a space for the intended use or when media center space is used for purposes for which it was not designed.

404. *An Analytical Study of the Recommendations of Early Childhood Education Authorities with Regard to the Role of the Public Library in Serving Children from Infancy to Six Years of Age*, by Frances A. Smardo. ERIC 1978. ED 160222.

Report results of a study on the named topic, with the facilities section providing six basic recommendations.

405. "Blueprint for Action," by Elizabeth T. Fast. *School Media Quarterly* 2(1974): 194-199. Reprinted in *Media Center Facilities Design*, compiled and edited by Jane A. Hannigan and Glenn E. Estes. Chicago: American Library Association, 1978. 26-30.

Discusses the importance of maintaining parallel planning of media center facilities and media programs. The author feels that in order for a facility design to be successful it must match the needs of the programs that will take place within it. Includes a detailed chart showing the individual steps of the two parallel processes and a bibliography.

406. "Children and Territory in a Library Setting," by Irene Sever. *Library and Information Science Research* 9.2(1987): 95-103.

Reports the results of a study of children's sense of territoriality in a physically unstructured library environment. Includes tables and a bibliography.

407. *Children's Services of Public Libraries*, edited by Selma K. Richardson. Papers presented at the Allerton Park Institute, 23rd, Monticello, Illinois, November 13-16, 1977. Urbana: Graduate School of Library Science, University of Illinois, 1978. ERIC ED 167129.

Provides overview of the status of children's services in public libraries. Includes "Library Facilities for Children," by Margaret Bush, which is treated separately in this bibliography.

408. "Community Study and Building Programs for School Media Centers," by F. William Summers. *Media Center Facilities Design*, compiled and edited by Jane A. Hannigan and Glenn E. Estes. Chicago: American Library Association, 1978. 34-36.

Looks at the importance of involving school media personnel in the facilities design process and proposes the use of a formal building program as one means of achieving this level of participation.

409. *Considerations Before Writing a Public Library Building Program in Children's Services*, by Faith Hektoen. Hartford: Connecticut State Library, 1978. ERIC ED 207570.

Provides guidelines for preparation of building programs

for children's areas. Includes review of types of behaviors observed in children's rooms, suggestions for creating formulas to determine collection size, audiovisual area requirements, shelving and storage of children's materials, space and interior design requirements for different age children and different functional areas.

410. "Design Considerations." *Media Center Facility Design for Maryland Schools*. Baltimore: Division of Library Development and Services, Maryland State Department of Education, 1975. 13-20. Reprinted in *Media Center Facilities Design*, compiled and edited by Jane A. Hannigan and Glenn E. Estes. Chicago: American Library Association, 1978. 49-54.

Provides detailed guideline checklist for school media center facilities design. Topics covered include aesthetics, safety, environment, acoustics, utilities and furnishings. Also looks at planning functional areas, including reading, studying, viewing and listening, large group, office and media planning, seminar or activity, production and processing, darkroom, storage and videotaping.

411. "Designing a Library/Media Resource Center," by Charles Vlcek. *Singapore Libraries* 12(1982): 56-60.

Reviews the importance of the role of the librarian/media professional in the overall facility design process. Includes illustrations.

412. "Designing Student Production Facilities," by Richard Gilkey. *School Media Quarterly* 2(1974): 256-259. Reprinted in *Media Center Facilities Design*, compiled and edited by Jane A. Hannigan and Glenn E. Estes. Chicago: American Library Association, 1978. 71-72.

Briefly looks at the facility requirements for the production of super-8mm film, video, still photographs, and audio recordings.

413. "Facilities Planning," by Joyce B. Scholl. *The School Library Media Program: Instructional Force for Excellence*, by Ruth Ann Davies. 3rd edition. New York: R.R. Bowker, 1979. 535-547.

> This is an appendix on school library facilities planning, consisting of checklists and worksheets. Topics covered include the reception or circulation area, general use area, special use areas, work/storage areas, production areas, proposed agenda for staff meeting on facility design and a sample facility layout. Each of these broad areas also include consideration of such specific points as space requirements, furniture, etc.

414. "Libraries are Relaxants," by Edward Kuhlman. *Clearing House* 55.2(1981): 88-89.

> Author argues for a return to simple school library design with the emphasis on a dignified and spartan approach, rather than the current styles which he classifies as flashy.

415. "Library Consultant: Who? When? Why?," by Kenneth R. Shaffer. *School Media Quarterly* 2(1974): 221-223. Reprinted in *Media Center Facilities Design*, compiled and edited by Jane A. Hannigan and Glenn E. Estes. Chicago: American Library Association, 1978. 213-216..

> Reviews the role and activities of consultants when planning and designing media centers. Looks at what the consultant does, how to select and hire a consultant, and how fees can be handled.

416. "Library Facilities for Children," by Margaret Bush. *Children's Services of Public Libraries*. Paper presented at the Allerton Park Institute, 23rd, Monticello, Illinois, November 13-16, 1977. Urbana: Graduate School of Library Science, University of Illinois, 1978. 109-117. ERIC ED 167729.

> Provides broad overview of children's facilities in public

libraries. Topics covered include use of color, properly sized furnishings, the learning environment, layout and interior design, flexibility, storage space, traffic flow and the planning process. Includes a bibliography.

417. "Library Facilities for Children," by Diana Young. *Public Libraries* 18.3(1979): 71-73.

Looks at some of the major issues, trends, and challenges facing librarians planning libraries for children. Includes checklists of types of materials, furniture, space and design considerations. Also includes a bibliography.

418. "The Many Uses of Color in Library Rooms Serving Children," by Katherine Habley. *Illinois Libraries* 60(1978): 891-895.

Discusses the importance color plays in children's areas in libraries, with examples and recommendations of how to use colors to achieve desired design effects.

419. "Media and Facilities Design," by Gerald F. McVey. *Media Center Facilities Design*, compiled and edited by Jane A. Hannigan and Glenn E. Estes. Chicago: American Library Association, 1978. 72-85.

Detailed look at the planning and design of media center facilities. Topics covered include general considerations and guidelines, learning spaces, small and medium group spaces, multi-use facilities, centralized media centers, projection systems and viewer requirements, lighting, color, acoustical control, sound systems, temperature and seating. Includes tables, illustrations and a bibliography.

420. "Media Center Aesthetics," by Walter Dziura. *School Media Quarterly* 2(1974): 287-294. Reprinted in *Media Center Facilities Design*, edited by Jane A. Hannigan and Glenn E.

Estes. Chicago: American Library Association, 1978. 57-60.

Reviews the importance of layout, furnishings and color in creating an environment conducive to learning. Includes a bibliography.

421. *Media Center Facilities Design*, compiled and edited by Jane A. Hannigan and Glenn E. Estes. Chicago: American Library Association, 1978.

This collection of previously published materials includes the following papers that are treated separately in this bibliography, "Personal space and the media center," by Estelle Jussim, "Persons and environment," by Kay E. Vandergrift, "Student views: an exploratory research design," by Jane A. Hannigan and Kay E. Vandergrift, "A report of research on student views," by Jane A. Hannigan and Kay E. Vandergrift, "Blueprint for action," by Elizabeth T. Fast, "Some prior questions," by Donald P. Ely, "Ten commandments for media center planners," by Elizabeth P. Hoffman, "Community study and building programs for school media centers," by F. William Summers, "Planning process and trade-offs," by Gerald Proderick and Stephan Langmead, "Facilities," by AASL and ALA, "Applying the T square between program and facilities," by Estella E. Reed, "Design considerations," by the Maryland State Department of Education, "State funding and local planning for school construction," by Estelle B. Williamson, "Media center aesthetics," by Walter Dziura, "But where do I plug the carrel in?" by Gaylen B. Kelley, "Designing student production facilities," by Richard Gilkey, "Media and facilities design," by Gerald F. McVey, "Media center facilities: a photographic essay," by Elnora M. Portteus, "Library consultant," by Kenneth R. Shaffer, "Merged facilities: potential and constraints," by Mae Graham and J. Maurice Travillian, "After the architect's gone for his reward," by Peggy Sullivan, "Individualized learning through media," by Zatha A. Tallman, and "Edsels, behemoths, or transfiguration: restoration and renovation of media facilities," by Lynne M. Birlem and Arthur

C. Gillis.

422. "...Of Shoes, and Ships and Ceiling Racks...: New Ideas of Children's Facilities," by Paula Sinclair. *Illinois Libraries* 60(1978): 880-884.

Looks at the different perspectives of administrators and children's librarians in terms of architectural planning for children. Advocates the active participation of librarians on planning and design committees so that the special needs of children can be met.

423. *Pathfinder: An Operational Guide for the School Librarian,* by Patricia Freeman. New York: Harper and Row, 1975.

Includes ·chapter on facility planning, design and construction. Topics covered include the planning process, siting, noise control, appearance, light, air quality, security, furniture and equipment. Includes a bibliography.

424. "Personal Space and the Media Center," by Estelle Jussim. *School Media Quarterly* 2(1974): 189-193. Reprinted in *Media Center Facilities Design,* compiled and edited by Jane A. Hannigan and Glenn E. Estes. Chicago: American Library Association, 1978. 7-10.

Provides an overview of media center space planning, with an emphasis on the psychological aspects of the topic. The article discusses crowding, differing needs of individuals, staff needs, the media center environment and finance.

425. "Persons and Environment," by Kay E. Vandergrift. *School Media Quarterly* 4(1976): 311-316. Reprinted in *Media Center Facilities Design,* compiled and edited by Jane A. Hannigan and Glenn E. Estes. Chicago: American Library Association, 1978. 10-13.

Looks at the psychological and social aspects of media center facilities planning.

426. "Planning Process and Trade-Offs," by Gerald Prodrick and Stephan Langmead. *Media Center Facilities Design,* compiled and edited by Jane A. Hannigan and Glenn E. Estes. Chicago: American Library Association, 1978. 36-40.

Discusses the implications of cost-benefit analysis in planning current and future facility requirements for media centers. Topics covered include designing for the future, flexibility and the ability to change, modular planning, building configuration, fixed vs. modular planning, standard components vs. custom designed, tile vs. carpet and lighting. Includes a table.

427. "Planning School Media Centers," by Tom A. Teeter. *NASSP Bulletin* 59(1975): 41-46.

Overview of school media center planning. Looks at program development, environmental considerations, and furniture and equipment. Includes a brief bibliography.

428. "Public Library Services for Young Children," by Frances A. Smardo. *Children Today* 9(1980): 24-27.

Within the overall context of children's services in public libraries, this article contains a brief list of facilities guidelines.

429. "Relationships Between Literature Programs, Library Corner Designs, and Children's Use of Literature," by Lesley M. Morrow. *Journal of Educational Research.* 75(1982): 339-344.

Analyzes the physical characteristics of library corners in nursery, kindergarten, first and second grade classrooms and correlates those characteristics with the the frequency of use of literature by nursery and

kindergarten children. Includes tables giving data
analyses and a bibliography.

430. "A Report of Research on Student Views," by Jane A.
Hannigan and Kay E. Vandergrift. *Media Center Facilities
Design,* compiled and edited by Jane A. Hannigan and Glenn
E. Estes. Chicago: American Library Association, 1978.
18-25.

Reports the results of a study designed to evaluate the
opinions of students on their school media centers.
Includes tables giving data analyses, conclusions and
recommendations. (see "Student Views: An Exploratory
Research Design," in this bibliography for a discussion
of the research design used in this study.)

431. "School Library Building, Furniture and Equipment," by
Rajwant Singh. *International Library Movement* 4.3-4(1982):
54-59.

Reviews basic design factors important in planning,
designing, and constructing a school library. Also looks
at relevant Indian standards.

432. *School Library Media Centers.* Austin: Texas Education
Agency, 1985. ERIC ED 263916.

Guide to the planning, evaluation and improvement of
school library media centers. Facilities sections include
broad overview of general requirements, as well as
specific standards (for each of four different levels of
LMC's) for the following: circulation, viewing, listening
and reading, small group viewing and listening,
conference, maintenance and repair, media production,
dark room, professional collection, stacks, microcomputer,
magazines and newspapers, and administrative areas. A
"Library Media Center Checklist," with a section on
facilities is included. The report also has a brief
bibliography. Other states have also prepared this type
of report and these can be accessed through ERIC.

433. "Some Prior Questions," by Donald P. Ely. *School Media Quarterly* 4(1976): 317-322. Reprinted in *Media Center Facilities Design*, compiled and edited by Jane A. Hannigan and Glenn E. Estes. Chicago: American Library Association, 1978. 30-32.

Looks at the concept of school media center design using the open-plan space approach, including both the advantages and disadvantages. Includes a brief bibliography.

434. "State Funding and Local Planning for School Construction," by David R. Bender and Estelle B. Williamson. *School Media Quarterly* 2(1974): 217-220. Reprinted in *Media Center Facilities Design*, compiled and edited by Jane A. Hannigan and Glenn E. Estes. Chicago: American Library Association, 1978. 54-56.

Describes the funding program for school libraries in Maryland. Looks at the overall plan of operation, media staff involvement, requirements for functional areas and space planning. Includes a table.

435. "Student Views: An Exploratory Research Design," by Jane A. Hannigan and Kay E. Vandergrift. *Media Center Facilities Design*, compiled and edited by Jane A. Hannigan and Glenn E. Estes. Chicago: American Library Association, 1978. 14-18.

Reports the planning and design of a study aimed at evaluating student opinions of their school media centers. The article includes details on sampling, methodology, the instruments, data analysis and evaluation. (see "A Report of Research on Student Views" in this bibliography for the results of this study.)

436. "Teachers and the School Resource Centre," by Shirley Blair. *Canadian Library Journal* 35(1978): 93-100.

Looks at the factors which influence how teachers use the school resource center, including a consideration of the affect of facilities.

437. "Ten Commandments for Media Center Planning," by Elizabeth P. Hoffman. *School Media Quarterly* 2(1974): 223-226. Reprinted in *Media Center Facilities Design,* compiled and edited by Jane A. Hannigan and Glenn E. Estes. Chicago: American Library Association, 1978. 32-34.

Lists and discusses ten basic guidelines for planning school media center facilities.

438. "Trends in School Library Media Facilities, Furnishings, and Collections," by Jim Bennett. *Library Trends* 36(1987): 317-326.

Part of a special issue on library buildings, this article provides an overview of recent and continuing trends in the planning and construction of school library facilities. Looks at traffic flow design considerations, the relationships of function, behavior and aesthetics, impact of new electronic media, use of space, color, lighting and access for the handicapped. Includes traffic flow drawings and a bibliography.

1.4.3 Evaluation or Description of Actual Facilities

439. "A Children's Branch in the Bedroom," by Aud Nordgarden and Gunnar Westgard. *Scandinavian Public Library Quarterly* 11.2(1978): 33-35.

Reports on the use of two bedrooms in suburban houses as temporary children's libraries in Bodo, Norway. This approach was undertaken because the new suburbs are too far from existing libraries located in the center of the older town. Contains illustrations.

440. "Individualized Learning Through Media," by Zatha A. Tallman. *School Media Quarterly* 2(1974): 274-279. Reprinted in *Media Center Facilities Design*, compiled and edited by Jane A. Hannigan and Glenn E. Estes. Chicago: American Library Association, 1978. 105-108.

> Describes the planning and design of the library media center at Corona del Mar High School in Newport Beach, California. Includes layout drawings.

441. "Library Logistics," by Claudia Karas and Janet Koop. *Early Years* 10(1979): 43.

> Describes the design and construction of a very small school library (8.5' by 9').

442. "Media Center Facilities: A Photographic Essay," by Elnora M. Portteus. *School Media Quarterly* 2(1974): 203-212. Reprinted in *Media Center Facilities Design*, compiled and edited by Jane A. Hannigan and Glenn E. Estes. Chicago: American Library Association, 1978. 90-93.

> Includes annotated photographs of seven school media centers.

443. "A Media Center for the 21st Century," by Bernice Lamkin. *School Library Journal* 33.3(1986): 25-29.

> Looks at the planning and design of a high school media center in Michigan.

1.4.4 Renovations and Additions

444. "Edsels, Behemoths, or Transfiguration: Restoration and Renovation of Media Facilities," by Lynne M. Birlem and Arthur C. Gillis. *School Media Quarterly* 2(1974): 268-273.

Reprinted in *Media Center Facilities Design,* compiled and edited by Jane A. Hannigan and Glenn E. Estes. Chicago: American Library Association, 1978. 108-111.

> Reviews the planning and design process that can be used when renovating an existing media center. Includes a sample planning chart.

445. "Let's Redesign the Library: A Simulation Game," by Linda D. Olsen. *Audiovisual Instruction* 23(1978): 41-42.

> Describes simulation activity involving teachers, administrators and students used to redesign an intermediate school library in California.

446. "The Planning and Modification of Library Media Center Facilities," by Naomi W. Butler and Yale Stenzler. *Drexel Library Quarterly* 13.2(1977): 62-79.

> Describes the process of planning and implementing the renovation of library media centers. Topics covered include the library media program, the planning process, responsibilities of system and building level personnel, budgets, educational specifications, schematics, design development and construction documents, furniture and equipment, evaluation and design considerations in renovation. Includes a planning steps checklist, a time chart, and a brief bibliography.

447. "Remodeling the Library," by Aaron Cohen and Elaine Cohen. *School Library Journal* 24.6(1978): 30-33.

> Part of a special issue on library building renovation and conversion, this article provides suggestions for different types of renovations that can be done in school libraries. Topics covered include color, acoustics, floor coverings, lighting, traffic flow, layout and estimating time requirements. Also gives guidelines for a remodeling proposal document to be given to school administrators. Includes illustrations.

1.5 Special Libraries

1.5.1 Bibliographies, Standards, History and Multiple-Library Statistical Overviews

448. "A Bibliography on Library Planning," by Janice A. Kreider. *Planning the Special Library*, edited by Ellis Mount. (SLA Monograph no. 4) New York: Special Libraries Association, 1972. 80-94.

> An annotated bibliography which covers the topics of proceedings, general books and articles, preplanning, the planning team, specifications and bidding, remodeling, lighting, air conditioning, fire protection, flooring, design and layout, furniture, shelving, equipment, map equipment, copying equipment, microform equipment, security, automation, moving and case studies. Most citations are to materials published before 1970.

449. "Building, Furniture and Equipment for Special Libraries," by Rajwant Singh. *Herald of Library Science* 21(1982): 227-238.

> Reviews relevant Indian standards for special library facilities. Also looks a the basic elements involved in planning, designing and constructing a special library, including requirements for functional areas, furniture and equipment.

450. "Standards for Education Libraries," by Helen R. Rockman. *Education Libraries* 6(1981): 61-62.

> Reviews work of the Committee on Standards for Educational Library Services of the Educational and Behavioral Sciences Section of the Association of College and Research Libraries of ALA. Includes three basic areas which should be considered when formulating facilitates standards for education libraries. Also includes a bibliography.

1.5.2 Planning a Facility: General Considerations

451. "Accommodation," by Muriel Anderson. *Manual of Law Librarianship: The Use and Organization of Legal Literature*, edited by Elizabeth M. Moys. London: Andre Deutsch, 1976. 602-626.

> This chapter looks at the major factors to be considered when designing law libraries, including the proportion of serials to monographs and the need to retain older materials. Also considers the topics of shelving, user space, signage and security requirements. Includes illustrations and a bibliography.

452. "Archives Buildings: International Comparisons," by David Thomas. *Journal of the Society of Archivists* 9(1988): 38-44.

> Examines and analyzes the factors which have influenced the design of archival buildings outside the UK and compares the resulting buildings with UK archival facilities. Includes a bibliography.

453. "A Checklist with Guidelines for Library Planning," by Jeanette S. Rockwell and Jean E. Flegal. *Planning the Special Library*, edited by Ellis Mount. (SLA Monograph no. 4) New York: Special Libraries Association, 1972. 59-79.

> This very detailed checklist covers the broad topics of the library environment, analyzing the library operations and planning the program, the planning team, research and investigation of the experience of others, preparation of the building program, equipment and furniture planning and layout, and moving of library materials and equipment.

454. "The Design of Archives Buildings," by Bernard Faye. *UNESCO Journal of Information Science, Librarianship and Archives* 4(1982): 88-93.

Examines problems related to the design of archives facilities. Includes discussion of programming difficulties, site selection, open vs. closed access, and air conditioning and energy conservation. Includes layout drawings and a very brief bibliography.

455. "Guidelines for Planning Facilities for Sci-Tech Libraries," by Howard Rovelstad. *Science and Technology Libraries* 3.4(1983): 3-19.

Part of a special issue on library facility planning, this article gives an overview of the planning, design, and construction processes involved in creating a new or renovated facility. Includes the role of the librarian, use of a planning committee, selection of an architect, use of consultants, the building program and making space requirements projections. Also includes a bibliography.

456. "Hospital Libraries," by Godfrey Thompson. *Architects' Journal* 163(1976): 595-598.

Reviews the design problems found in many hospital libraries, which the author largely ascribes to the failure of librarians to consult either design professionals or use hospital library standards. Includes suggested layouts for different situations. Includes illustrations and a bibliography.

457. *Hospital Library Management*, edited by Jane Bradley. Chicago: Medical Library Association, 1983.

Within the context of a broad-based overview of managing hospital libraries, this work includes one chapter titled "Planning library facilities," by Jacqueline Bastille, which is treated separately in this bibliography. Other topics covered include hospital library standards, selecting, acquiring and organizing library materials, providing library services, managing library services, and providing special services.

458. "Library Functions and Their Relationship to Space Design," by Bettie J. Third. *Planning the Special Library*, edited by Ellis Mount. New York: Special Libraries Association, 1972. 49-51.

Discusses the use of functional relationship planning aids and design approaches in special libraries. Includes a sample relationship diagram.

459. "Library Planning, Furniture, and Equipment," by Alderson Fry. *Handbook of Medical Library Practice*, edited by Gertrude L. Annan and Jacqueline W. Felter. 2nd edition. Chicago: Medical Library Association, 1970. 284-330.

Covers how to plan the library, library size and shape, lights and ceiling, floors and floor loading, flow patterns, entrances and exits, circulation area, reserve area, receiving area, staff work spaces, housing the collection, housing the users, carrels, special purpose rooms, noise control, the building program, interior design and furnishings, expanding and remodeling, moving, use of consultants and legal concerns. Includes an extensive bibliography.

460. *Manual for Prison Law Libraries*, by O. James Werner. (American Association of Law Libraries publication no. 12) South Hackensack: Rothman, 1976.

Intended for nonprofessionals, this manual includes a discussion of facility requirements. Includes a bibliography.

461. *National Library Buildings*, edited by Anthony Thompson. Proceedings of the Colloquium held in Rome, 3-6 September 1973. (IFLA Publications 2) Pullach/Munchen: Verlag Dokumentation, 1975.

Reports on conference on national library buildings, with papers in English or French. Topics covered include the program for a national library, the function of national libraries and the impact on building design, libraries in the USSR, Canada's new National Science Library building and civic planning problems.

462. "Physical Access to Resources," by Irwin H. Pizer and William D. Walker. *Handbook of Medical Library Practice,* edited by Louise Darling. 4th edition. vol. 1. Chicago: Medical Library Association, 1982. 15-64.

General discussion of access related issues including security, collection arrangement, stacks and storage, theft detection systems and handicapped access. Includes floor layout and a bibliography.

463. "Planning and Maintenance of Library Facilities and Resources," by Clara A. Robeson. *Library Practice in Hospitals: A Basic Guide,* edited by Harold Bloomquist, et al. Cleveland: Case Western Reserve University, 1972. 147-171.

This chapter reviews the fundamentals of planning, designing and constructing library facilities in hospitals. Topics covered include space requirements, the user area, the work area, photocopying area, lighting, floors and floor coverings, ceilings, walls, windows, ventilation, shelving, periodical shelving, furniture, supplies and maintenance procedures. Includes illustrations, layout drawing and a bibliography.

464. "Planning Library and Information Services," by L.J. Anthony. *Handbook of Special Librarianship and Information Work.* 4th edition. London: Aslib, 1982. 3-71.

This chapter reviews facility planning for special libraries. Topics covered include the design of systems, measurement techniques, user studies, physical planning, functional relationships, space requirements, standards, layout, expansion and convertibility, shelving, compact shelving, furniture, audiovisual materials, accessibility, orientation, lighting, acoustics, interior design and moving. Includes numerous illustrations, layout drawings and a bibliography.

465. "Planning Library Facilities," by Jacqueline Bastille.
Hospital Library Management, edited by June Bradley.
Chicago: Medical Library Association, 1983. 265-294.

Detailed look at planning hospital library facilities.
Topics covered include responsibility for space planning,
planning for additional space, estimating general space
requirements, estimating space requirements by
functional area, making a detailed space estimate,
preparing planning documents, choosing between new
construction or remodeling, designing and constructing
library facilities, moving the library and planning for
the future. Appendices include space formulas and a
sample space estimate for a library in a 200-bed
community hospital (ten year projection). Includes a
layout of functional areas, floor plans, and a
bibliography.

466. "The Planning Team," by Bette Snyder. *Planning the
Special Library*, edited by Ellis Mount. (SLA Monograph no.
4) New York: Special Libraries Association, 1972. 45-48.

Reviews how a planning team can be used in the
special library facility planning process. Topics covered
include the relationship of the librarian and the parent
organization management, the architect and the
consultant. Includes a brief bibliography.

467. *Planning the Administrative Library*, by David Overton.
(IFLA Publication 26) New York: K.G. Saur, 1983.

Discusses the planning of governmental special libraries
(administrative) in an international context. Topics
covered include administrative organization and its effect
on library structure, library planning, first decisions,
library service points, location of the library within the
building complex, general access area, work areas,
storage and ancillary services, lighting, heating, air

conditioning, solar gain, acoustics, furniture, shelving, floor coverings, color schemes, mechanical aids and planning ahead. Includes a bibliography.

468. "Planning the Law Firm Library," by James O. Smith. *Planning the Special Library*, edited by Ellis Mount. (SLA Monograph no. 4) New York: Special Libraries Association, 1972. 55-58.

Provides basic criteria and guidelines, including general considerations, layout, staff facilities, books and tables, and lighting.

469. "Planning the Library for Use," by Anne Collins. *Medical Librarianship*, edited by Michael Carmel. London: The Library Association, 1981. 153-170.

This chapter on facilities planning includes the topics of space requirements, location, public areas, staff areas, housing the collection, layout, lighting, equipment and signage. Includes illustrations, layout drawings and a bibliography.

470. *Planning the Special Library*, edited by Ellis Mount. (SLA Monograph no. 4) New York: Special Libraries Association, 1972.

Includes 15 papers on library facility planning, with the following 12 treated separately in this bibliography, "Space utilization in a special library: making do with what you get," by Gordon E. Randall, "Structural requirements of library planning," by Robert Beder, "Interior design: beauty is our excuse," by Mary Nikas, "Miscellaneous library equipment and floor coverings," by Elizabeth J. Gibson, "Wood furniture in the library," by S.S. Coston, "Metal library equipment," by C.L. Rice, "The planning team," by Bette Snyder, "Library functions and their relationship to space design," by Bettie J. Third, "Library moving procedure," by Jane A. Schuyler, "Planning the law firm library," by James

O. Smith, "A checklist with guidelines for library planning," by Jeanette S. Rockwell and Jean E. Flegal, and "A bibliography on library planning," by Janice A. Kreider. The book also includes descriptions and layouts for seven special libraries.

471. *Religious Archives: An Introduction*, by August R. Suelflow. Chicago: Society of American Archivists, 1980.

This manual includes guidelines for facilities planning and requirements. Includes bibliography.

472. *Running a Library: Managing the Congregation's Library With Care, Confidence, and Common Sense*, by Ruth S. Smith. Greenwich: Seabury, 1982.

Within the broad context of establishing and maintaining a church or synagogue library, this manual contains a section on space planning and facility design.

473. "Space Planning for the Information Unit of an Industrial Organization," by A.K. Anand and H.R. Chopra. *International Library Movement* 6.1(1984): 1-8.

Provides space utilization guidelines for a corporate information center and discusses various factors which can impact space allocation and layout. Includes tables, illustrations, and a bibliography.

474. "Space Utilization in a Special Library: Making Do with What You Get," by Gordon E. Randall. *Planning the Special Library*, edited by Ellis Mount. (SLA Monograph no. 4) New York: Special Libraries Association, 1972. 6-12.

Reviews the inadequate space problems often faced by special librarians. Discusses a process that can be used to calculate projected future space and collection requirements. Includes tables, layout drawings and a brief bibliography.

475. "Special Libraries," by Giuliana Lavendel. *Chemical and Engineering News* 55.16(1977): 34-42.

Within broad context of science special libraries, this article discusses the use of remote storage and establishing a magnetic tape library.

476. *Special Libraries and Information Centers: An Introductory Text*, by Ellis Mount. New York: Special Libraries Association, 1983.

Within the broad topic of special libraries, this book includes sections on planning library facilities and equipment. Topics covered include planning, design considerations, moving, storage and layout. Includes illustrations and a bibliography.

477. *A Theological Library Manual*, by Jannette E. Newhall. London: The Theological Education Fund, 1970.

Provides chapter on the library building, including coverage of location and general architecture, services, building consultants, materials shelving and storage requirements, housing the reader, layout, circulation desk, staff areas, storage areas, building materials, lighting and renovations.

478. "Trends in Special Library Buildings," by Elaine Cohen and Aaron Cohen. *Library Trends* 36(1987): 299-316.

Part of a special issue on library buildings, this article discusses recent and continuing trends in the planning and construction of special library facilities. Emphasis is given to the growing role of online and telecommunications systems, the growth of corporate and governmental "campuses" and the development of special library systems. Also discusses space requirements and standards, and furniture and equipment. Includes a chart, illustrations, and floor plans.

1.5.3 Evaluation or Description of Actual Facilities

479. "The Alexander Library Building, Perth, Western Australia," by David Hickson. *Australian Library Journal* 34.3(1985): 5-20.

> Describes the planning, design, and construction of a large state library building. Topics covered include the program, architects, construction planning, consultants, parking garage, project documentation, layouts and space planning, furniture planning and control, color, equipment, signage, and moving the library. Includes basic portions of the program and photographs.

480. "Alexandria Updated: The Brief for the British Library Building, Euston Road, London," by David T. Rodger. *Aslib Proceedings* 31(1979): 314-321.

> Reviews the history and development of the facility, including a brief discussion of the major points included in the program. Also reviews the process of developing and implementing the program.

481. "Brunschwig and Fils Archives," *Interior Design* 53(1982): 292-294.

> Describes planning and construction of an archives facility for an interior design company. Includes a floor plan and photographs.

482. "British Library Starts on Site." *Architects Journal* 14(1982): 56-58.

> Describes the design process for the British Library building, including the use of computer-aided-design, the use of deep basements for storage, contract organization and steps taken to reduce the chance of ground movement. Includes illustrations and a bibliography.

483. "China's New National Library," by Basil Stuart-Stubbs. *Quill and Quire* 53.12(1987): 18.

Looks at the new national library building in Beijing, including a description of the architectural design and features. Includes an illustration.

484. "Design of Library Facilities for the Ontario Ministry of Transportation and Communications," by Stefanie A. Pavlin, et al. *Science and Technology Libraries* 3.4(1983): 43-50.

Part of a special issue on planning library facilities, this article looks at the planning, design, construction, and move of a governmental special library. Includes illustrations and a brief bibliography.

485. "Efficiency and Library Space," by Paula M. Strain. *Special Libraries* 70(1979): 542-548.

Reports the process used to redesign the existing special library of the MITRE Corporation in McClean, VA, in order to make better use of the available space. Includes illustrations.

486. "A Hospital Library Building Program," by Emilie Lightfield, et al. *Bulletin of the Medical Library Association* 64(1976): 41-44.

Looks at the process used to design and implement the building program of the library at Christ Hospital in Cincinnati in Ohio. Includes examples, sections of the program and a table.

487. The Law Library Company of Philadelphia: Oldest Law Library Gets a New Home." *Library Journal* 95(1970): 4146-6147.

Describes the architectural design and interior layout of the oldest American law library.

488. "The Libraries of the Los Alamos National Laboratory," by Lois E. Godfrey. *Science and Technology Libraries* 7.1(1986): 57-65.

> Looks at a very large technical library facility, including planning, layout and features, and compromises and post-occupancy changes. Includes basic architectural and space usage statistics, a photograph and a layout drawing.

489. *The Library of Congress: Its Architecture and Decoration,* by Herbert Small. New York: Norton, 1982.

> A revision of the 1901 publication, this work discusses the planning and construction of the Library of Congress, together with detailed descriptions of the interior decoration. Includes numerous photographs.

490. "The NDL's Annex Building: A Pictoral Sketch." *National Diet Library Newsletter* 74/75(1986): 1-5.

> Brief description of the new annex at the National Library of Japan. Includes several pictures of the new facility.

491. "A New Pharmaceutical Company Library: The Upjohn Company Corporate Technical Library," by Lorraine Schulte. *Science and Technology Libraries* 7.1(1986): 15-29.

> Looks at a new large (25,000 square feet) corporate library. Describes the planning process, with special attention to technology-related factors. Includes basic architectural and space usage statistics, a photograph, and a layout drawing.

492. "Prison Libraries: A Consumer's Point of View," by Geoffrey Hall. *Assistant Librarian* 75.11(1982): 147-148.

> Describes the prison library facilities at Strangeways

Prisons, Manchester, England.

493. "The Urquhart Building of the British Library Lending Division: The Design of a Single Function Library Building," by E.S. Smith. *Interlending Review* 9.2(1981): 50-56.

Part of a special issue on planning special science and technology libraries, this article describes the staged building program used to plan and construct a building devoted exclusively to interlibrary loan, including the use of special mechanical materials transportations systems. Includes illustrations and a brief bibliography.

494. "A Whaling Library for Massachusetts: Report From New Bedford," by Joan Ackerman. *Wilson Library Bulletin* 56(1981): 100-104.

Describes the library addition to the Whaling museum. Use of space, a conservation laboratory, environmental control, and shelving of special materials are discussed.

1.5.4 Renovations and Additions

495. "Adapting an Ancient Archives Building in Turin," by Isabella Massabo and Marco Carassi. *Information Development* 4.1(1988): 37-40.

Looks at the conversion and renovation of an eighteenth century palace to house a modern state archives collection. Topics covered include architectural restoration, enlarging the storage facilities, lighting, heating and cooling, climatization and fire protection. Includes illustrations.

496. "Adaptive Reuse of Old Buildings for Archives," by Jay Haymond. *American Archivist* 45(1982): 11-18.

Describes the renovation of a railroad depot to become quarters for the Utah State Historical Society. Reviews the advantages of adaptive reuse of older structures, the programming process, environmental control, building code requirements, costs and problems of working with architects and builders.

497. "Efficiency and Library Space," by Paula M. Strain. *Special Libraries* 70(1979): 542-548.

Describes the renovation of the MITRE Corporation Library in McLean, Virginia. Discusses the planning of the renovation, the roles of the librarian, architect and contractor, and the actual renovation. Includes floor plans and photographs.

2.0 HOUSING AND SERVING THE USER, STAFF AND COLLECTION

2.1 Reader/Staff Areas and Furnishings: General Considerations

498. "Application of Queueing Network Models to Optimization of Resource Allocation Within Libraries," by J. MacGregor Smith and William B. Rouse. *Journal of the American Society for Information Science* 30(1979): 250-263.

> Discusses how floor plans and library activities can be used to construct a network queueing model as a means of arriving at the optimal distribution of patron service demands.

499. "Appropriate Settings for Reference Service," by Robert Pierson. *Reference Services Review* 13.3(1985): 13-30.

> Describes 13 desired architectural characteristics of the reference area in libraries. Includes discussion of space requirements for materials, staff and new technology devices. Includes illustrations and a bibliography.

500. *Centralization of Current Periodicals at the University of Missouri at Columbia,* by June Weese and Michele Reiling. ERIC, 1976. ERIC ED 153605.

> Reports a feasibility study on centralizing periodicals in order to provide increased accessibility, reduce theft and

improve technical service productivity. Includes current and proposed periodical area layouts.

501. "The Chair Tables the Motion: A Special *AL* Report on Library Furniture." *American Libraries* 19(1988): 261-261-272, 297-307.

Includes five brief articles on new developments in library furniture which are treated separately in this bibliography. These are "Kick the legs," by Lee B. Brawner, "A critical survey," by Andrea A. Michaels, "Office landscape systems," by Gloria Novak, "Surprise and delight," by Ben Weese and "Great American chair competition," by Suzy M. Conway. Also includes eight page photo layout of new furniture.

502. *Circulation and Library Design: The Influence of "Movement" on the Layout of Libraries,* by D.L. Marples and K.A. Knell. Cambridge: Kings College, Cambridge University, 1971.

Reviews role of interior layout in increasing user satisfaction with the library by controlling traffic flow to produce quiet areas. Authors feel that appearance is often of too much concern to library designers. Includes layout drawings of "quiet area" design approaches.

503. "Compensatory Reaction to Spatial Intrusion: An Examination of Contradictory Findings," by E. R. Mahoney. *Sociometry* 38(1975): 420-427.

Discusses research methodology designed to study the reactions of library users to the presence of other users, particularly when seated at reading tables. Includes a bibliography.

504. "Design for Users," by Andrea Michaels. *Wilson Library Bulletin* 62.1(1987): 56-59.

Looks at the use of adjustable furniture in the library, with general guidelines, keyboard and display support surfaces, seating, angles between back and seat, armrests, casters, footrests, power, and selection. Includes ergonomic drawings.

505. "Design Today," by Andrea Michaels. *Wilson Library Bulletin* 61.6(1987): 34-35, 79.

Discusses the role of the interior designer in successful facility design. Covers what a designer can be expected to do and how to select one.

506. "Designed for Users," by Nolan Lushington. *Wilson Library Bulletin* 56(1981): 125-127.

Discusses the factors to be considered when selecting various types of seating for the library. Describes several major types and manufacturers.

507. "Designing a Reference Station For the Information Age," by Margaret Becket and Henry B. Smith. *Library Journal* 111.7(1986): 42-46.

Discusses the process used to design a new reference station for the main library at the University of Rochester. A list of seven "wishes" is given, together with the solutions for each need. Includes follow-up evaluation after a year of use, list of eight conclusions, floor plans, photographs, a layout and a bibliography.

508. "Designing the Perfect Reference Desk," by Joyce M. Crooks. *Library Journal* 108(1983): 970-972.

Describes process of designing a reference work station. Such factors as what tasks will be performed, what equipment is required, physical characteristics of staff and patrons, traffic patterns, flexibility of placement, available space and style of reference service are reviewed. Includes ergonomic drawing of the desk, layout of the workstation area, drawing of the workstation, and a bibliography.

509. "The Ecology of Study Areas," by Robert Sommer. *Environment and Behavior* 2(1970): 272-280.

Reports results of research study examining how college students on 23 campuses choose their study areas, including libraries. Includes table giving data analyses, and a bibliography.

510. "Environmental Design Applications," by Marjorie A. Lyles. *Special Libraries* 63(1972): 495-501.

Overview of the importance of such environmental factors as color, light, sound, layout, and furniture in the effective utilization of the library by the user. The article focuses on special libraries, but the points apply to all types. Includes photographs and a bibliography.

511. "Environmental Psychology: Factors in Library Environments," by William H. Ittelson. *The User Encounters the Library: An Interdisciplinary Focus on the User/System Interface*, edited by Martin B. Steffenson and Larry D. Larason. Proceedings of a Library Training Institute, Monroe, Louisiana, July 31-August 3, 1978. Monroe: Northeast Louisiana University, 1986. 1-18. ERIC ED 266791.

Provides a brief introduction to environmental psychology, with limited direct reference to library situations. Transcriptions of participant questions do provide library specific points in such areas as privacy, social interaction, personalization of space, windows, external approaches to library (landscaping and lighting), color and environmental psychologists as building consultants.

512. "Evaluating the Strength of Library Chairs and Tables,"

by Carl A. Eckelman. *Library Technology Reports* 13(1977): 341-433.

Detailed examination of different design approaches to library furniture. Topics covered include concepts of design strength, classification and structural characteristics of chair and table support systems, performance expectations and service loads, library table evaluation, library chair evaluation and examples of design. Includes tables and numerous illustrations.

513. *Furnishing the Library Interior,* by William S. Pierce. New York: Marcel Dekker, 1980.

Detailed overview of designing and furnishing the library interior. Topics covered include the planning process, the planning team, consultants, housing the user, housing services and staff, housing the collection, housing nonprint media, selection, evaluation and purchase of library furniture and equipment, manufacture and marketing of library furniture and equipment, interior appointments and systems. Includes photographs, drawings, sample specifications, and a bibliography.

514. "Furnishings Can Surprise and Delight," by Ben Weese. *American Libraries* 19(1988): 272, 297-298.

Part of a special report on library furniture, this article advocates the strong involvement of the librarian in the furnishings design and selection process. Includes photographs of multi-level carrels.

515. "The Great Library Chair Contest," by Suzy M. Conway. *American Libraries* 19(1988): 299.

Reports how students, faculty and a library staff participated in a contest designed to compare several different new proposed chairs for an academic library. Includes a photograph.

5.16. "Human Factors of Queuing: A Library Circulation Model," by Jerry W. Mansfield. *Journal of Academic Librarianship* 6(1981): 342-344.

Looks at the application of queuing theory combined with an appreciation for human factors in developing successful building layouts. Includes a brief bibliography.

517. "Human Needs and Working Places," by Robert Propst. *Running Out of Space: What are the Alternatives?*, edited by Gloria Novak. Papers from a Preconference at the American Library Association Annual Meeting, 1975. Chicago: American Library Association, 1978. 139-144.

Looks at the psychological aspects of facility design, for both public and staff areas.

518. "Improving Library Effectiveness Through a Sociophysical Analysis," by Karen Ambrose and Lawrence Ambrose. *Bulletin of the Medical Library Association* 65(1977): 438-442.

Reports a study conducted at the Christ Hospital Evangelical School of Nursing in Oak Lawn, Illinois that evaluated the library's physical environment and found it to be a major negative factor in the library's overall effectiveness. After the library was rearranged, faculty and students reported a higher level of satisfaction with both the librarians and the library. Includes illustrations, tables and a brief bibliography.

519. "Interior Design: Beauty is Our Excuse," by Mary Nikas. *Planning the Special Library*, edited by Ellis Mount. (SLA monograph no. 4) New York: Special Libraries Association, 1972. 18-25.

Reviews the roles interior designers can play in the planning and design process. Topics covered include space planning, budgeting, furnishings, bid documents, working with an interior designer, special problems for special libraries and the design product.

520. *Interior Design Factors in Library Facilities,* by Patricia A. Jackson. Dallas: Texas Woman's University, 1979. ERIC ED 174207.

Looks at the basic factors to be considered when planning library interiors, including use of design principles, psychological reactions of patrons to the design, color, light, functional requirements, comfort, efficiency, and the handicapped.

521. *Interior Design for Libraries,* by James Draper and James Brooks. Chicago: American Library Association, 1979.

Review of the principles involved in interior design and how they can be successfully applied in a variety of library environments. Chapter topics include using professionals, planning, movement flow, color, fabric, walls, windows, floors, space allocation and organization, displays and purchasing. Includes photographs, layouts, glossary, and a bibliography.

522. "The Interior Designer," by Marshall Brown. *Talking Buildings: A Practical Dialogue on Programming and Planning Library Buildings,* edited by Raymond M. Holt. Proceedings of a Building Workshop, Pasadena, California, October 3-4, 1985. Sacramento: California State Library, 1986. 35-39. ERIC ED 271109.

Reviews purpose of interior designer in facility design process. Includes selection guidelines and detailed examination of the expected functions of interior designer.

523. "Kick the Legs...," by Lee B. Brawner. *American Libraries* 19(1988): 263-265.

Part of a special report on library furniture, this

article reviews current trends and how some older elements of library furniture design are making a comeback. Other topics briefly covered include the use of new technologies, tendency of public libraries to adopt academic library approaches, compact shelving and basic policy decisions on furniture selection and acquisition. Includes a brief bibliography.

524. "Library Design Influences on User Behavior and Satisfaction," by David E. Campbell and Theodore M. Schlechter. *Library Quarterly* 49(1979): 26-41.

Reports research study using three different methodologies to determine the influence of library design on academic library user behavior and satisfaction. Includes tables and a bibliography.

525. "Library Furniture," by D.R. Grover. *Indian Library Movement* 5(1978): 65-76.

Discusses the importance of acquiring high quality library furniture, which should be attractive, durable and functional. Looks at standards for different types of library furniture. Includes a bibliography.

526. "Library Use, Library Instruction, and User Success," by Beth J. Shapiro and Philip M. Marcus. *Research Strategies* 5.2(1987): 60-69.

Presents the results of a study looking at how people use academic libraries. Findings include evaluation of the role of physical facility design in user success.

527. "Metal Library Equipment," by C.L. Rice. *Planning the Special Library*, edited by Ellis Mount. (SLA Monograph no. 4) New York: Special Libraries Association, 1972. 34-36.

Reviews the various types of metal furniture and equipment used in libraries and provides guidelines for their selection. Includes photographs.

528. "Miscellaneous Library Equipment and Floor Coverings," by Elizabeth Gibson. *Planning the Special Library*, edited by Ellis Mount. (SLA Monograph no. 4) New York: Special Libraries Association, 1972. 26-30.

Reviews design considerations and requirements for a variety of furnishings, including study carrels, periodical display racks, circulation desks, card catalogs, sinks, book trucks, ladders and floor coverings. Includes photographs.

529. "Music Cataloging in Academic Libraries and the Case for Physical Decentralization: A Survey," by Annie F. Thompson. *Journal of Academic Librarianship* 12(1986): 79-83.

Reports the results of a study investigating cataloging in academic music libraries, including the centralization of the process and the physical location of the cataloger. Includes tables giving data analyses and a bibliography.

530. "Noise Reduction in an Undergraduate Library," by Charles P. Bird and Dawn D. Puglisi. *Journal of Academic Librarianship* 10(1984): 272-277.

Reviews the noise reduction procedures undertaken at Ohio State University, which included space reallocation, behavior rules and staff monitoring. Includes tables.

531. "On Reading in Modern Libraries," by Bernhard Fabian. *LIBER Bulletin* 16(1981): 10-15. Proceedings of a Seminar held in Heidelberg in November, 1980 on library architecture.

Part of a special proceedings issue on library architecture, this article looks at the deficiencies present in many current academic libraries from the user's perspective. Relevant factors identified include inadequate privacy, lighting and air conditioning. Includes a brief bibliography.

532. "Patron Preference in Reference Service Points," by Linda Morgan. *RQ* 19(1980): 373-375.

Contrasts patron preferences for desk or counter furniture arrangements at reference service points. Includes drawings and tables.

533. "Perceptions of Crowding and Pleasantness in Public Settings," by Lou McClelland and Nathan Auslander. *Environment and Behavior* 10(1978): 535-553.

Reports research studying relationship of crowding and "pleasantness" in various settings, including libraries. Includes tables giving data analyses and a bibliography.

534. "Personal Space and Facilities Usage," by Robert Sommer. *The User Encounters the Library: An Interdisciplinary Focus on the User/System Interface,* edited by Martin B. Steffenson and Larry D. Larason. Proceedings of a Library Training Institute, Monroe, Louisiana, July 31-August 3, 1978. Monroe: Northeast Louisiana University, 1986. 1-17. ERIC ED 266791.

Reviews basic concepts of human spatial needs as they impact library facility design. Areas covered include variety, flexibility and personalization of space. Emphasis given to seating/spacing patterns, relationship of furniture types to space utilization (particularly carrels), non-standard seating approaches, eating facilities and location and design of the reference desk.

535. "Problems of the Open Space Library," by Stephan R. Hildrich. *Connecticut Libraries* 20(1978): 42-44.

Discusses the problems associated with libraries designed using an open space approach, including both patron and staff dissatisfaction. Includes a bibliography.

536. "Quiet vs. Noisy Patrons: Erecting Noise Barriers."
Library Journal 104(1979): 145-146.

Describes methods that can be used to minimize noise
in libraries, including glass enclosed rooms and
spreading out of furniture. Also reviews the various
levels of noise that can be accommodated in different
parts of libraries. Includes a layout drawing.

537. "Reducing Noise in a College Library," by Paul D.
Luyben, et al. *College and Research Libraries* 42(1981):
470-481.

Reports the results of a library noise reduction study
and project at the State University of New York
College at Cortland. The study design and methodology
are provided. Includes floor plans, noise level charts
and an extensive bibliography.

538. "The Reference Desk: Service Point or Barrier?" by
Larry Larason and Judith Schiek. *RQ* 23(1984): 332-338.

Reviews factors in optimal placement of the reference
desk, including communication and promotion, layout,
positioning and personal space. Provides "approachability
model" which is tested. Includes a bibliography.

539. "Seating and Area Preferences in a College Reserve
Room," by Diane Fishman and Ruth Walitt. *College and
Research Libraries* 33(1972): 284-297.

Reports a research study examining the relationship
between the architectural environment of a reserve
reading room and the seating pattern preferences of
users. Includes tables, layout floor plans, and a
bibliography.

540. "Standard Lines or Custom Designed?" by Andrea A. Michaels. *American Libraries* 19(1988): 267-269.

Part of a special report on library furniture, this article discusses the past failures of library furniture designers and manufacturers and follows with a discussion of how some of the current companies are overcoming these past problems. Includes photographs.

541. "Too Close for Comfort: Sex Differences in Response to Invasions of Personal Space," by Jeffrey D. Fisher and Don Byrne. *Journal of Personality and Social Psychology* 32(1975): 15-21.

Reports a research study of how males and females sitting at tables in a university library react to other users sitting down and working at the same table. Includes tables giving data analyses and a bibliography.

542. "Toward the Environmental Design of Library Buildings," by Lamar Veatch. *Library Trends* 36(1987): 361-376.

Part of a special issue on library buildings, this article examines various aspects of environmental design in libraries, including environmental psychology, privacy, proxemics and personal space, territoriality, and ergonomics and human factors. Includes a bibliography.

543. "Trends in Staff Furnishings for Libraries," by John Vasi. *Library Trends* 36(1987): 377-390.

Part of a special issue on library buildings, this article reviews recent and continuing trends in furniture for use by library staff. Topics covered include service desks, terminals, chairs, work surfaces, panels, desk lamps, anti-glare screens, copy holders and footrests in staff work areas. Also looks at office areas. Includes a brief bibliography.

544. "The University Library: An Important Setting for the Study of Environment-Behavior Relationships," by David E. Campbell and Theodore M. Schlechter. *Man-Environment Systems* 8(1978): 41-42.

Reports a research study performed at the main library of the University of Kansas, that examined the distribution of user behavior in different parts of the library, areas of satisfaction and dissatisfaction and user traffic patterns.

545. "Use of Performance Tests and Quality-Assurance Programs in the Selection of Library Chairs," by Carl A. Eckelman. *Library Technology Reports* 18(1982): 479-581.

Discusses the factors used in the performance evaluation of library chairs, with special attention given to user behavior towards furniture. Examines various specific testing approaches and how the resulting data can be used. Includes tables, illustrations, and a bibliography.

546. *Use of Personal Space in Libraries: A Review*, by Gulten Wagner. ERIC, 1983. ERIC ED 267806.

Literature review of personal space research, particularly as it relates to libraries. Studies are examined in eight areas: seating preference, relationship of spatial nearness and emotional reactions, use of carrels, use of models in personal space research, boundary changes and adjustments, development of personal space models, roles of culture, gender and age in space utilization, and role of personalities in space utilization. Includes an extensive bibliography.

547. *The User Encounters The Library: An Interdisciplinary Focus on the User/System Interface*, edited by Martin B. Steffenson and Larry D. Larason. Proceedings of a Library Training Institute, Monroe, Louisiana, July 31-August 3, 1978. Monroe: Northeast Louisiana University, 1986. ERIC

ED 266791.

Papers presented by speakers from disciplines such as sociology, psychology, criminal justice and marketing. Facilities related papers that are treated separately in this bibliography include "Anticipating needs of users," by Edward P. Miller, "Environmental psychology: factors in library environments," by William H. Ittelson, "Personal space and facilities usage," by Robert Sommer, "Deviant behavior in the library," by Dale Welch, and "Architectural approaches to design and behavior," by Nancy McAdams. Includes an overview bibliography and transcripts of the participant discussions.

548. "Users Come First in Design," by Philip M. Bennett. *Wisconsin Library Bulletin* 74(1978): 51-58. Reprinted in *The Mainstreamed Library: Issues, Ideas, Innovations*, edited by Barbara H. Baskin and Karen H. Harris. Chicago: American Library Association, 1982. 25-30.

Considers physiological considerations in the design of library facilities. Topics covered include visual response to the environment (light, color, brightness, sitting positions), thermal response, auditory response, tactile response, and psychological and sociological considerations in design. Includes ergonomic diagrams.

549. "What Color Should We Paint the Walls?" by Emily Muir. *North Country Libraries* 13(1970): 1-4.

Provides general review and guidelines on selection of wall coverings based on such factors as proportion, clutter, light, and focus.

550. "Wood Furniture for the Library," by S.S. Coston. *Planning the Special Library*, edited by Ellis Mount. (SLA Monograph no. 4): New York: Special Libraries Association, 1972. 31-33.

Looks at the basic criteria that should be used to select wood furniture. Includes photographs.

551. "Work Spaces, Satisfaction, and Productivity in Libraries," by Jeanne M. Isacco. *Library Journal* 110.8(1985): 27-30.

Reviews the literature and research of non-library fields on the topic of staff work spaces, then relates these findings to their potential impact on optimal staff working conditions in libraries. Includes a bibliography.

2.2 Reader/Staff Areas and Furnishings: Nonprint Materials

552. *Accessible Storage of Nonbook Materials*, by Jean Weihs. Phoenix: Oryx Press, 1984.

Presents a discussion and recommendations for storing a wide variety of nonbook materials. Also includes illustrations and an extensive annotated bibliography.

553. *An Annotated Bibliography of Slide Library Literature, Bibliographic Studies no. 3*, by Stanley W. Hess. Syracuse: School of Information Studies, Syracuse University, 1978. ERIC ED 181926.

An broad literature review of current (1960-1978) materials dealing with nonbook librarianship. Facilities section includes 15 partially annotated entries.

554. *Audio-Visual Space Reorganization Study: RDU-75-05*, by Martha Baker. Lafayette: Purdue University, 1975. ERIC ED 112927.

Reports the analysis of space layout and workflow patterns in the Audiovisual Center at Purdue

University, with details of proposed changes. Current and future layouts, and present and planned space requirements are provided.

555. *Audiovisual Media in the Dutch Public Library*, by Ed Spruit. Translated by Michael Mann and Joni Mann-Schipper. The Hague: Netherlands Bibliotheek en Lektuur Centrum, 1983. ERIC ED 269008.

Reports a five year study of seven Dutch public libraries on the integration of audiovisual materials into existing collections. The chapter on library layout includes consideration of furniture, shelving and electrical power supply.

556. *Developing Microform Reading Facilities*, by Richard W. Boss and Deborah Raikes. Westport: Microform Review, Inc., 1981.

General guide to planning, designing and implementing microform facilities, including space requirements for materials and people, types of microformats and equipment. Includes illustrations, tables and a bibliography.

557. *Film Library Techniques: Principles of Administration*, by Helen P. Harrison. New York: Focal Press Limited, 1973.

Includes chapter on storage and preservation of film, including the need for separate storage facilities, vaults, temperature, humidity, ventilation and storage equipment. Also covers the different functional areas of the library and how they should be placed in relationship to each other. The book includes a bibliography.

558. *Guidelines for Audiovisual Materials and Services for Large Public Libraries*. Chicago: Public Library Association, American Library Association, 1975.

Includes guidelines on storage and equipment.

559. "An Inexpensive Horizontal Map Storage Facility," by Joseph J. Gerencher. *Geography and Map Division Bulletin (SLA)* 141(1985): 2-6.

Describes the planning and construction of a new map storage facility using moveable horizontal shelving in the science library of Moravian College in Pennsylvania. Includes illustrations.

560. *Map Librarianship*, by Harold Nichols. Hamden: Linnet Books, 1976.

A chapter on storage provides a discussion and suggestions for the special requirements of different types of cartographic materials. The book includes a bibliography.

561. *Map Study Committee. Final Report*, by Bob Heidlage, et al. Columbia: Missouri University Library, 1980. ERIC ED 195255.

Reports the results of a study made of an academic library map collection in order to make forecasts about facilities, equipment and personnel needs. Includes specifications of storage and access space requirements. Also includes tables and a bibliography.

562. *Microform Librarianship*, by S.J. Teague. London: Butterworths, 1977.

Includes a chapter of the microform reading room. Topics covered include basic equipment, siting of facilities, minimum requirements and layout. Includes floor plans and a brief bibliography.

563. "Microform Room Environments: The External Factors,"

by Arthur C. Tannenbaum. *Serials Librarian* 5.3(1981): 25-34.

Looks at the facility considerations of planning microform rooms, including lighting, temperature, acoustics, aesthetics and space requirements. Includes a bibliography.

564. "Microforms and the User: Key Variables of User Acceptance in a Library Environment," by Susan K. Nutter. *Drexel Library Quarterly* 11.4(1975): 17-31.

Overview of a process designed to gain user acceptance of microforms. Facility related topics include the physical and psychological environment, storage and handling, equipment and the general microform area. Includes a bibliography.

565. "Microforms at Princeton," by Deborah A. Raikes. *Microform Review* 11.2(1982): 93-105.

Reports on a project designed to improve microform services and facilities at Princeton. Includes coverage of capital improvements, equipment, storage, layout and costs.

566. *Microforms in Libraries: A Manual for Evaluation and Management,* edited by Francis Spreitzer. Chicago: American Library Association, 1985.

Includes brief consideration of facilities, storage and environmental factors associated with microforms. Includes a glossary, a list of standards, specifications and a bibliography.

567. "Physical Planning for Map Libraries: The Process," by Gloria Novak. *Western Association of Map Libraries Information Bulletin* 13.1(1981): 23-29.

Proposes . a process used to define and solve storage and space related problems in map libraries.

568. "Planning a Microform Center for the Art Library," by Evelyn Samuel. *Microform Review* 8.3(1979): 160-163.

Overview of the specific requirements for microforms in an art library, including spatial functional relationships, patron and staff participation in the planning process, cost, environmental requirements, furniture, equipment and services.

569. "Public Library Buildings and AV Services: A Draft of a Medium-Sized Public Library Layout," by Jan Wallinder. *Scandinavian Public Library Quarterly* 18.4(1985): 97-99.

Presents guidelines for the effective use of modern audiovisual technologies in the library, particularly in the areas of telecommunications and electrical power. Based on a study of a Swedish library system, this article suggests placing audiovisual services very near the library entrance. Includes illustrations.

570. "Sabbatical Report: Results of a Survey of Library Microforms Facilities," by Melinda C. McIntosh. *Microform Review* 16.1(1987): 40-51.

Reports results of a survey of the microform facilities in 11 academic libraries. Looks at facilities factors and signage as well as several non-facility design related factors. Includes tables.

571. *Shelving Capacity in the Music Library,* by Robert M. Fling. (MLA Technical Report no. 7) Philadelphia: Music Library Association, 1981.

Overview and discussion of shelving requirements for different formats in the music library, including books, scores and recordings. Includes numerous tables and formulas. Also includes an extensive bibliography.

572. *Slide Libraries: A Guide for Academic Institutions, Museums, and Special Collections,* by Betty Jo Irvine. 2nd edition. Littleton: Libraries Unlimited, 1979.

Within the broad context of slide librarianship, this book includes chapters on storage and access systems and planning for physical facilities. Topics covered include selection of a storage facility, types of storage, environmental control, functional space requirements (storage, viewing, circulation and reference, administration and operation, storage, and photography and processing), floor plans and preparing a building program. Includes drawings, photographs, a building program for a slide library at Indiana University, floor plans, a spatial relationships drawing, and bibliographies.

573. "Space and Planning," by Patricia del Mar. *How to Start an Audiovisual Collection,* edited by Myra Nadler. Metuchen: Scarecrow Press, 1978.

Reviews facility design considerations for functional areas, including public service, circulation, media storage, offices, work areas, film screening areas, individual viewing areas and production areas. Includes a brief bibliography.

574. "The Storage and Handling of Videocassettes in Libraries," by Murray Weston. *Audiovisual Librarian* 8.1(1982): 31-33.

Provides temperature, humidity and magnetic field storage guidelines for videocassettes.

575. "Storage of Photographs in Libraries," by Sandy Eaglestone. MLS Thesis. Loughborough University of Technology (n.d.).

Provides detailed storage guidelines for photographic collections. Includes tables, illustrations and a bibliography.

576. "Time-Space and the Music Library, by Mary Wallace. *Music Library Association Notes* 27(1970): 12-18.

Looks at shelving and storage requirements for the different formats of materials found in music libraries.

577. "User Environment and Attitudes in an Academic Microform Center," by Arthur Tannenbaum and Eva Sidhom. *Library Journal* 101(1976): 2139-2143.

Looks at ways of improving user attitudes toward microforms by means of changing various facility design related environmental factors.

578. "User Environment in a Microform Center," by Arthur Tannenbaum and Eva Sidhom. *Library Space Planning: Issues and Approaches* (*LJ* Special Report no. 1, edited by Karl Nyren) New York: R.R. Bowker, 1976. 36-37.

Discusses the environmental factors considered in the development of New York University's Bobst Library Microform Center, as well as the process used to respond to these factors. Topics covered include centralization, humidity, lighting, carrels and staff areas.

579. "User Preference Studies of Microfiche: The M.I.T. Project Intrex and Barker Engineering Library Experiences," by Susan K. Nutter. *Running Out of Space: What Are the Alternatives?*, edited by Gloria Novak. Proceedings of a Preconference at the American Library Association Annual Meeting, 1975. Chicago: American Library Association, 1978. 32-46.

Describes the planning, design and use of a "model library", including specially designed microform areas, used to conduct a number of user preference studies. Includes a transcription of a discussion by preconference participants.

580. "Vertical Map Storage," by Joanne Perry. *Special Libraries* 73(1982): 207-212.

Advocates the use of vertical, rather than traditional horizontal, storage of maps. Includes illustrations.

581. "A View From the Outside," by Godfrey Thompson. *Audiovisual Librarian* 8.2(1982): 62-66.

Looks at the planning and design of audiovisual library facilities, including open and closed stacks, security, acoustics and lighting.

2.3 Stack and Storage Areas

582. *An Analysis of Book Storage and Transportation Requirements of the Five Associated University Libraries,* by Tesfaye Dinka and Davut Okuctu. Syracuse: Five Associated University Libraries, 1970. ERIC ED 049767.

Reports the results of a study designed to produce a storage/transportation model for book materials. Topics covered include land and construction cost data, library space data and delivery systems cost data. Data was analyzed to compare three storage systems (conventional, Yale, Randtriever), as well as alternative methods of interlibrary transportation. Includes data analysis tables and a bibliography.

583. "The Annex Library of Princeton University: The Development of a Compact Storage Library," by Lucinda Conger. *College and Research Libraries* 31(1970): 160-168.

Describes an open stack approach to compact storage.
Looks at the construction of the building and the
shelving plan. Also covers the program and service
related topics. Includes a bibliography.

584. *Book Storage in Academic Libraries: A Report Submitted
to the Council on Library Resources,* by George Piternick.
ERIC, 1974. ERIC ED 112835.

Reports results of a study of book storage in large
North American academic libraries. Within the general
context of storage, the report provides a brief look at
storage facilities, together with general recommendations.

585. *Capital Provision for University Libraries: Report of a
Working Party.* London: Her Majesty's Stationery Office,
1976.

Reports a British study of stack and storage
requirements in university libraries. Includes
questionnaire, methodology, recommendations, formulas,
tables and charts.

586. "Compact Shelving," by Frazer G. Poole. *Running Out
of Space: What are the Alternatives?,* edited by Gloria Novak.
Preconference at the American Library Association Annual
Meeting, 1975. Chicago: American Library Association, 1978.
49-57.

Gives an overview of compact shelving, with brief
descriptions of typical configurations and setups. The
author makes the point that in his experience, compact
shelving may save space but it does not result in
significant cost savings.

587. "Compact Shelving Specifications," by Charles R. Smith.
Library Administration and Management 1(1987): 94-95.

Provides a checklist of items to be considered when

writing specifications for compact shelving, based on a survey of 41 libraries that had recently installed such shelving. Also includes survey results and a list of companies that supply compact shelving.

588. "Comparing Costs," by Donald D. Thompson. *Bulletin of the American Society for Information Science* 7.1(1980): 14-15.

Examines and compares costs involved in using high density remote storage, weeding and conversion to microforms. The benefits of each are discussed.

589. "A Conversation with Robert J. Trelease," by Brian Alley. *Technicalities* 4(1984): 3-5, 15.

Interview with a library bookstack dealer, giving the background of the business and current developments and trends.

590. "A Cost Model for Storage and Weeding Programs," by Gary S. Lawrence. *College and Research Libraries* 42(1981): 139-147.

Presents cost model designed to simplify the complex decisions required in deciding whether to weed the materials collection or place items in a storage facility. Includes an example of the model's application at the University of California's libraries. Includes tables, a bibliography, and an appendix with mathematical details of the model.

591. "Curbing the Growth of Academic Libraries," by Daniel Gore. *Library Journal* 106(1981): 2183-2187.

Recommends the use of cooperative storage facilities for little used materials by academic libraries.

592. "Economic Characteristics of the Library Storage

Problem," by Richard A. Stayner. *Library Quarterly* 53(1983): 313-327.

Reports on a model based on storage and retrieval costs that permits optimal allocation of a collection to different types of storage approaches in academic libraries. Includes tables and a bibliography.

593. *An Economic Criterion for Housing and Disposing of Library Materials, Based on Frequency of Circulation.* (Research report RR-799-2) Sacramento: University of California, 1979. ERIC ED 191488.

This study reports the economic and academic advantages of using compact shelving to store infrequently used library materials as opposed to discarding them. Details of the cost model used are included, as is the study methodology.

594. *Farewell to Alexandria: Solutions to Space, Growth, and Performance Problems of Libraries,* edited by Daniel Gore. Westport: Greenwood Press, 1976.

This collection includes several papers dealing with facilities, including "Sizing up the space problem in academic libraries," by Claudia Schorrig, "Balbus; or the future of library buildings," by Ellsworth Mason, "Limiting college library growth: bane or boon?" by Evan Ira Farber, and "Solving space and performance problems in a public library," by Marvin Scilken. Includes illustrations, tables and bibliographies.

595. "Floor Loading Problems in Academic Libraries," by David H. Eyman. *Library Administration and Management* 1(1987): 97-99.

Looks at the problems caused by floor loading inadequacies in libraries. Briefly reviews the basic standards and then follows with three brief case studies illustrating common situations. Includes a bibliography.

596. "From Attic to Annex: The Story of an Off-Campus Storage Facility," by Valerie J. Feinman. *Serials Librarian* 5.4(1981): 49-57.

Describes the planning and implementation of a remote off-campus materials storage facility at Adelphi University in New York. Also reviews in general the larger storage capacity problems facing libraries. Includes tables and a bibliography.

597. "Harvard University's Storage Experience," by Robert R. Walsh. *Running Out of Space: What are the Alternatives?*, edited by Gloria Novak. Proceedings of a Preconference at the 1975 American Library Association Annual Meeting. Chicago: American Library Association, 1978. 3-9.

Reviews the history of how Harvard has coped with the storage of its very large collections in a wide variety of facilities.

598. "Housing Books," by George S. Grossman. *Law Library Journal* 79(1987): 521-534.

Looks at different storage strategies as alternatives to building new law library buildings. Includes a bibliography and illustrations.

599. "An Interim Solution to an Overcrowded Academic Library," by Evelyn D. Regan. *California Librarian* 38(1977): 44-49.

Describes the remote storage facility at the Library of the California Polytechnic State University. Includes a floor plan of the storage area showing how the collection was organized.

600. "Making Space: Automated Storage and Retrieval," by Norman Tanis and Cindy Ventuleth. *Wilson Library Bulletin* 61.10(1987): 25-27.

Reports the planning, design and implementation of a large scale automated materials storage and retrieval system at California State University at Northridge. Includes illustrations.

601. "The Measurement and Projection of Shelf Space," by Ralph M. Daehn. *Collection Management* 4.4(1982): 25-39.

Reviews the literature concerned with measuring, monitoring, and forecasting library collection shelf space. Includes a detailed description of a survey conducted at the University of Guelph Library, with tables showing shelf space survey data for different types of materials, holdings conversion factor formulas and a bibliography.

602. "Measuring a Library," by P.G. Peacock. *Aslib Proceedings* 35(1983): 152-155.

Provides process to accurately estimate the amount of shelving currently in use in a library. Includes a brief bibliography.

603. "Microforms as an Alternative to Building," by Robert F. Asleson. *Running Out of Space: What are the Alternatives?*, edited by Gloria Novak. Proceedings of a Preconference at the American Library Association Annual Meeting, 1975. Chicago: American Library Association, 1978. 24-31.

Reviews the potential of using microform collections as a mechanism to solve storage space problems, thereby avoiding constructing or renovating facilities.

604. "An Observation on Shelving Practice," by Norman D. Stevens. *Library Journal* 103(1978): 1236.

Reports the result of a year long experiment based on comparing the approaches to shelving taken by two different academic libraries. Concludes that the practice of leaving the middle shelves empty for expansion cannot be recommended. Includes tables.

605. "Open Shelves/Closed Shelves in Research Libraries," by Mathilde V. Rovelstad. *College and Research Libraries* 37(1976): 457-467.

Presents arguments for and against open shelving in the research library. Cites the closed stack approach of German libraries as an appropriate model for U.S. libraries. Includes a bibliography.

606. "Open Stacks and Library Performance," by Harold B. Shill. *College and Research Libraries* 41(1980): 220-226.

Reports a six-year research study analyzing the transition from closed to open stacks at the main library at West Virginia University. Includes tables and a bibliography.

607. "Optimal Subdivision of Service Functions to Alternative Facilities Based on Usage Patterns: Application to Book Storage in University Libraries," by Bawa Jeet Singh. Dissertation. University of Cincinnati, 1977.

Proposes a general model designed to answer the questions "how much" and "what" materials to put in storage facilities. The model is tested using the University of Cincinnati Main Library.

608. "Planning for a Storage Facility at the University of Washington Libraries," by Margaret B. Tjaden. *Running Out of Space: What are the Alternatives?*, edited by Gloria Novak. Proceedings of a Preconference at the American Library Association Annual Meeting, 1975. Chicago: American Library Association, 1978. 10-20.

Reviews the history of how Washington has coped with serious materials storage problems, including the planning of a separate storage facility. Topics dealing with planning the facility include the site, building type, building size, shelving, bibliographical and physical access, costs, benefits of such a facility and current status of the project. Also includes a transcription of a discussion by preconference participants.

609. "Rare Books for Research: Separately Housed Collections," by John Bidwell. *Wilson Library Bulletin* 58(1983): 102-106.

Discusses the ramifications of housing rare books and special collections in a separate building.

610. "Regional Library Planning for Northern Campuses of the University of California," by Donald C. Swain. *Running out of Space: What are the Alternatives?*, edited by Gloria Novak. Proceedings of a Preconference at the American Library Association Annual Meeting, 1975. Chicago: American Library Association, 1978. 79-83.

Discusses the concept of regional libraries as a means of lessening space and storage problems, together with an evaluation of the advantages and disadvantages of the approach.

611. "Robots in the Library: Automated Storage and Retrieval Systems," by John Kountz. *Library Journal* 112(1987): 67-72.

Reviews recent advances in the application of automated storage systems and techniques in libraries. Topics covered include the benefits of such approaches, conservation considerations, physical appearance of systems, factors influencing size and costs. Includes tables, illustrations, and an annotated bibliography.

612. *Running Out of Space: What are the Alternatives?*, edited by Gloria Novak. Proceedings of a Preconference at American Library Association Annual Meeting, 1975. Chicago: American

Library Association, 1978.

Examines various storage alternatives for library
materials. Includes the following papers which are
treated separately in this bibliography, "Harvard
University's storage experience," by Robert R. Walsh,
"Planning for a storage facility at the University of
Washington Libraries," by Margaret B. Tjaden,
"Microforms as an alternative to building," by Robert
F. Asleson, "User preference studies of microfiche: the
MIT Project Intrex and Barker Engineering Library
experiences," by Susan K. Nutter, "Compact shelving,"
by Frazer G. Poole, "A truly automated retrieval
system, or compact storage a la carte," by Harold L.
Roth, "The new technology and the design of library
buildings," by Jack E. Brown, "Regional library
planning for northern campuses of the University of
California," by Donald C. Swain, "Problems of
renovating an existing library building," by Keyes
Metcalf, "University of British Columbia: The decision
to build an underground addition," by William Watson,
"The decision to build a new central library at the
University of Texas at Austin," by Nancy R.
McAdams, "Realities: funding of library construction," by
Kenneth E. Beasley, and "Human needs and working
places," by Robert Propst.

613. "Saving Space, Energy, and Money with Mobile
Compact Shelving: Georgetown University," by Joseph E.
Jeffs. *Library Space Planning: Issues and Approaches. (LJ
Special Report no. 1, edited by Karl Nyren)* New York: R.R.
Bowker, 1976. 38-40.

Describes the planning, installation, operation and
savings associated with a compact shelving system at
Georgetown University library.

614. "Sixth Stack Addition," by Martin H. Collier. *Library
Journal* 107(1982): 2235-2237.

Describes the Sixth Stack Addition to the General

Library at the University of Illinois, a facility custom-designed exclusively for multi-story, compact mobile book storage.

615. "A Solution for Too Many Books and Too Little Room," by Paul B. Huenemann. *The Library Scene* 10(1981): 14-16.

Describes the compact shelving system used at the University of Michigan at Dearborn library, emphasizing safety considerations and cost savings.

616. "Stack Capacity in Medical and Science Libraries," by Justine Roberts. *College and Research Libraries* 45(1984): 306-314.

Reports a stack capacity research study at the University of California health sciences and science libraries. Provides data for shelf capacity of serials, monographs and mixed shelving. Includes tables and a bibliography.

617. *Stack Management: A Guide to Shelving and Maintaining Library Collections*, by William J. Hubbard. Chicago: American Library Association, 1981.

Overview of collection and stack management. Topics covered include open shelves and stacks, shelving required for special formats (picture books, bound periodicals, unbound periodicals, rare books, cartographic, music, sound recordings, microforms, pamphlets, filmstrips, slides, kits, and art prints and sculpture), architectural potential of shelving, moving and shifting books, types of shelving, stack capacity, lighting, book transportation systems, signs, storage facilities (on-site, off-site, shared, cooperative) and storage shelving options (packed, compact, retrieval systems).

618. *To Grow or Not To Grow*, by John J. Boll. (*LJ* Special Report no. 15) New York: R.R. Bowker, 1980.

Discusses the alternatives that can be used to limit the increased need for space in academic libraries, including weeding, zero-growth, compact storage, coordinated acquisitions and miniaturization. Considers storage in terms of in-house vs. remote, cost, individual vs. cooperative storage and arrangement alternatives for stored materials. Includes a chart comparing several compact storage systems, photographs, and a bibliography.

619. "A Truly Automated Retrieval System or Compact Storage a la Carte," by Harold L. Roth. *Running Out of Space: What are the Alternatives?*, edited by Gloria Novak. Proceedings of a Preconference at the American Library Association Annual Meeting, 1975. Chicago: American Library Association, 1978. 58-64.

Gives a detailed look at an automated materials retrieval system developed for the Nassau County Research Library in New York. Includes a table contrasting the retrieval system, compact shelving and standard shelving.

620. *Ubibliotheca: The Spiral Library*, by Guy Ottewell. Urbana: Graduate School of Library Science, University of Illinois, 1970.

Describes a plan for a library with a storage level in the shape of a flat spiral, including a discussion of the advantages of such a design approach. Includes a floor plan, a section drawing and a bibliography.

2.4 Facilities for the Disabled

621. "Academia and Architecture: A Closer Look at Library Construction Relative to Section 504 Regulations," by Kathy Jackson and Marjorie Peregoy. *Dikta* 7.4(1983): 121-132.

Reviews basic requirements of Section 504 of the Rehabilitation Act of 1973. Reports the results of a research study examining the relationship between accessibility in academic libraries and the accessibility requirements of the Rehabilitation Act. Includes recommendations for further research, tables and a bibliography.

622. "Academic Library Service to Handicapped Students," by William M. Needham. *Journal of Academic Librarianship* 3(1977): 273-279.

Overview of problems encountered by the handicapped in academic libraries, with a brief discussion of facility related factors.

623. *Access II: A Guide to Massachusetts Post-Secondary Facility Libraries Serving Persons with Special Needs,* compiled by Thomas A. Ploeg and Judith M. Murphy. Boston: Massachusetts Board of Library Commissioners, 1978. ERIC ED 169707.

Directory of library facilities for the physically disabled in Massachusetts. Each entry includes geographic location, library name and address, contact person, special services for the physically disabled, specialized materials and equipment, accessibility both inside and outside the facility and information on policies dealing with individuals and groups not affiliated with the library. Includes index organized by the name of the library. Similar directories for other geographic and political entities can be accessed through ERIC.

624. *The Accessible Canadian Library: A Planning Workbook for a Barrier-Free Environment,* by Wendy Scott. Ottawa: National Library of Canada, 1986.

Provides detailed checklist of accessibility design features for library facilities. Covers specific functional areas such as circulation, the catalog, reference and the equipment required to support these functions. Also examines facility areas such as parking, walkways and passageways, entrances and exits, signage, doors, stairs, floors, ramps, handrails, elevators, restrooms, drinking fountains and telephones. Includes numerous diagrams and a bibliography.

625. *Architectural Accessibility for the Disabled of College Campuses*, by Stephen R. Colter and Alfred H. DeGraff. Albany: State University Construction Fund, 1976.

Guide to overall architectural accessibility guidelines for college and university facilities. The chapter on libraries provides standards for stack aisle widths, carrels, index and reference tables, telephones and signage, and entrances and doors. Guidelines are also given for wheelchair access, brace and crutch access, walks and curbs, ramps, wheelchair lifts, parking facilities, stairs, elevators, restrooms, residence halls, hallways, cafeterias, drinking fountains, walking surfaces, vending machines, performing arts, lecture halls, laboratories and alarm systems. Includes numerous charts and figures, together with an extensive bibliography.

626. "Architectural and Program Accessibility: A Review of Library Programs, Facilities, and Publications for Librarians Serving Disabled Individuals," by Ruth A. Velleman. *Drexel Library Quarterly* 16.2(1980): 32-47.

Provides overview of accessibility for the physically disabled. Facility related topics covered include definitions and attitudes, legislation, barrier-free library design and the National Center for a Barrier-Free Environment. Includes an annotated bibliography.

627. "Architectural Barriers," by Joan Goddard. *NNCL (News Notes of California Libraries)* 68(1973): 423-434.

Discusses problems associated with providing barrier-free access in library buildings. Also includes the

"Architectural Barriers: Library Building Survey" form which assesses such factors as off-street parking, passenger loading zones, entrance approaches, ramps and walks, entrance area, doors, elevators, stairs, floors, corridors and aisles, public restrooms, water fountains, public telephone, interior layout, mechanical system controls, identification for the visually handicapped, warning signals and hazards, resource and collection accessibility and library work factors.

628. "Archives: Accessibility for the Disabled," by Brenda B. Kepley. *American Archivist* 46(1983): 42-51.

Reviews reasons archivists should be concerned with handicapped access and looks at the needs of specific user groups. Provides an outline of a proposed process for improving accessibility in existing facilities.

629. "Barrier-Free Construction in Libraries," by Margery E. Hudson. *Current Studies in Librarianship* 2.1-2(1978): 46-52.

Reviews the major provisions of recent legislation dealing with barrier-free design, including the Architectural Barriers Act of 1968 and the Rehabilitation Act of 1973. Identifies eight major disability-related problems and their implications for library design. Specific standards for aisles, carrels, index and reference tables and entrances/exists in libraries are included. Additional general barrier-free standards covered include doorways, hallways, ramps, floor coverings, telephones, doorknobs, doors and signs. Seven site consideration factors are identified and discussed. Includes a bibliography.

630. *College and University Library Service for The Handicapped Student in Texas*, edited by James L. Thomas. Denton: North Texas State University, 1978. ERIC ED 1617165.

Directory of services, equipment and accessibility to

academic library facilities in Texas for the handicapped.
Each entry includes the library name, address,
telephone number, contact person, special equipment,
special services and a statement on the accessibility
situation. Similar guides for other geographic regions
are accessible through ERIC.

631. "Compact Shelving for MLC's Service for the
Handicapped," by Kathryn G. Merkle. *Dikta* 7.4(1983):
140-142.

Describes the planning and implementation of a compact
shelving system at the Mississippi Library Commission's
Service for the Blind and Physically Handicapped.

632. "Deny Access for the Disabled?" by Ronald H.
Gorsegner. *Wisconsin Library Bulletin* 74(1978): 59-60.

Reviews the architectural design requirements of
individuals in wheelchairs. Includes drawings giving
dimensions of wheelchairs, stair risers and recommended
door handles. Also includes a brief bibliography.

633. "Design Criteria for Educational Facilities for Special
Education Services," by Allen C. Aben. *Journal of Research
and Development in Education* 12(1979): 23-35. Reprinted in
Mainstreamed Library: Issues, Ideas, Innovations, edited by
Barbara H. Baskin and Karen H. Harris. Chicago: American
Library Association, 1982. 4-11.

Overview of problems associated with providing
appropriate facility design for the physically disabled.
Topics covered include placing standards for barrier-free
architecture in perspective, general building design
criteria, design criteria by environmental variable
(furniture) and design criteria by special educational
service.

634. "Design for Accessibility," by David R. Conn and Barry

McCallum. *Canadian Library Journal* 39(1982): 119-125.

Overview of accessibility problems in libraries. Reviews
the six major types of disabilities, site design, entrance
design, lighting, stairs and elevators, bookstacks,
equipment, furniture and security. Includes illustrations,
charts and a bibliography.

635. *The Disabled Child in the Library: Moving Into The
Mainstream*, by Linda Lucas and Marilyn H. Karrenbrock.
Littleton: Libraries Unlimited, 1983.

Within the broader context of the mainstreamed library,
this book includes a chapter on creating mainstreamed
environments. Topics covered include legislation and
standards, the planning process, common needs of all
children, basic rules for good design, furnishings,
lighting, acoustics, climate control, signage, safety,
conflicting needs and special problems of children with
mobility and dexterity disabilities. Includes a
bibliography.

636. "Disabled Libraries: An Examination of Physical and
Attitudinal Barriers to Handicapped Library Users," by
Robert T. Begg. *Law Library Journal* 72(1979): 513-525.
Reprinted in *The Mainstreamed Library: Issues, Ideas,
Innovations*, edited by Barbara H. Baskin and Karen H.
Harris. Chicago: American Library Association, 1982. 11-23.

Reviews the major ramifications associated with
providing barrier-free access in libraries. Topics covered
include laws, regulations and standards, professional
responsibilities, physical barriers, collection access and
utility, convenience and support facilities, costs and
attitudinal barriers. Includes an extensive bibliography.

637. "Fanciful and Functional: Illinois Regional Library,
Chicago." *Progressive Architecture* 59(1978): 76-81.

Looks at a library specifically designed for the blind

and physically handicapped, describing the physical disability related program considerations. Includes photographs, floor plans, three-dimensional projection drawings and architectural and construction data.

638. "The Handicapped and the Library Building," by Rannveig Eidet. *Scandinavian Public Library Quarterly* 14.2(1981): 41-42.

Reviews the legal requirements related to handicapped access in public libraries in Norway and the implications such regulations hold for all public library facility design.

639. "Hidden Barriers," by Suzanne Stephens. *Progressive Architecture* 59(1978): 94-97. Reprinted in *The Mainstreamed Library: Issues, Ideas, Innovations*, edited by Barbara H. Baskin and Karen H. Harris. Chicago: American Library Association, 1982. 31-34.

Discusses the psychological aspects of barrier-free design.

640. *Library and Information Services for Handicapped Individuals*, by Keith C. Wright and Judith F. Davie. 2nd edition. Littleton: Libraries Unlimited, 1983.

Within broader context of libraries and the physically disabled, this book discusses specific accessibility issues, standards, and guidelines for facility design, layout, furniture, shelving, elevators, etc. Includes "Suggested Revised Accessibility Checklist" and a bibliography.

641. "Library Facilities for the Disabled," by Monte Little. *Assistant Librarian* 74.11(1981): 140-143.

Looks at how special design considerations were made for the handicapped at a public library in Salisbury, England. Includes illustrations and a bibliography.

642. *Library Service to the Deaf and Hearing Impaired,* by Phyllis I. Dalton. Phoenix: Oryx Press, 1985.

Within the context of the broad topic of library service for the hearing impaired, this book includes one chapter on the environmental setting for such service. Topics covered include the use of signs in the library, elevators, lighting, acoustics, safety, meeting rooms, work accommodations for staff members, office design considerations, and cost and implementation of accommodations. Includes a bibliography.

643. *Library Signs and the Disabled,* by Marjorie A. Benedict. ERIC, 1979. ERIC ED 2221162.

Provides general guidelines to be used in developing and evaluating sign systems designed to be used by physically handicapped patrons. Discusses the International Symbol of Access and signage standards for libraries. Includes a copy of an instrument used to evaluate such sign systems. Also includes illustrations and a bibliography.

644. *The Mainstreamed Library: Issues, Ideas, Innovations,* edited by Barbara H. Baskin and Karen H. Harris. Chicago: American Library Association, 1982.

Within the broad context of the topic, this book includes one section on the physical environment. The following papers in this section are treated separately in this bibliography: "Design criteria for educational facilities for special education services," by Allen C. Aben, "Disabled libraries: an examination of physical and attitudinal barriers to handicapped library users," by Robert T. Begg, "Sensory wall brings learning," by Geraldine M. Matthews, "Users come first in design," by Philip M. Bennett, and "Hidden barriers," by Suzanne Stephens.

645. *Maryland Public Library Services for the Handicapped. A*

Survey for Handicapped Accessibility to Public Library Facilities. Baltimore: Division of Library Development and Services, Maryland State Department of Education, 1980. ERIC ED 208842.

> A directory identifying equipment, services and facilities available to handicapped library users in 24 Maryland public library systems. Similar directories for other geographic regions are accessible through ERIC.

646. "New Jersey Library for the Blind and Handicapped: Accessibility," by Deborah T. Rutledge. *Dikta* 7.4(1983): 103-108.

> Describes how accessibility concerns were addressed and met in the planning and construction of the Library Center for the Blind and Handicapped at the New Jersey State Library. Areas reported on include the availability of suitable public transportation, the building entrance, reader service areas, radio reading service area and additional public areas. Includes illustrations and tables.

647. *Planning Barrier Free Libraries: A Guide for Renovation and Construction of Libraries Serving Blind and Physically Handicapped Readers.* Washington, D.C.: National Library Service for the Blind and Physically Handicapped, Library of Congress, 1981.

> Considers accessibility problems by looking at such topics as planning prerequisites, selecting an architect, funding, the planning program, site selection, programming, schematic design, design development, working with consultants, drawings, contracts, barrier-free design, agency approvals, construction and renovations. Includes appendices on minimum space and personnel required, restroom requirements, flow diagrams, accessibility checklist and construction time schedules. Also includes numerous illustrations.

648. "Planning the Alabama Library for the Blind and Handicapped," by Charles A. Moss. *Dikta* 7.4(1983): 99-103.

Describes how the architects, the library director and the proposed head of the library cooperated to determine the major design elements of a library specially developed for the handicapped. Areas given special consideration include entry and reception, patron areas, administration, audiovisual materials storage, shipping and receiving, restrooms, lounge, elevators and mechanical systems.

649. *Revised Standards and Guidelines of Service for the Library of Congress Networks of Libraries for the Blind and Physically Handicapped 1984.* Chicago: American Library Association, 1984.

Gives the 1984 revision of the *Standards,* including two facility related standards. The "Guidelines" section contains a detailed set of space requirements for shelving, reader areas, staff areas and materials formats.

650. "Sensory Wall Brings Learning ," by Geraldine M. Matthews. *Wisconsin Library Bulletin* 74(1978): 181-182, reprinted in *The Mainstreamed Library: Issues, Ideas, Innovations,* edited by Barbara H. Baskin and Karen H. Harris. Chicago: American Library Association, 1982. 23-24.

Describes a wall treatment designed to enhance the sensory experiences of developmentally disabled patrons.

651. *That All May Read: Library Services for Blind and Physically Handicapped People.* Washington, DC: National Library Service for the Blind and Physically Handicapped, Library of Congress, 1983.

Composed of 15 papers giving an in-depth overview of the topic, including facility design issues. Includes very extensive bibliographies.

652. "The Wheelchair-Bound: Some Problems They Face in Libraries," by B. Krishnan. Thesis. Loughborough University of Technology, 1983.

> Gives overview of the layout and design difficulties faced by wheelchair bound individuals in libraries. Includes a bibliography.

653. "The Wolfner Move: 166 Tons and Wha'd'ya Get?," by Richard T. Miller. *Show-Me Libraries* 33.11(1982): 24-27.

> Describes the Wolfner Memorial Library for the Blind and Physically Handicapped in Missouri, including new facilities designed to serve the handicapped user. Includes illustrations.

2.5 New Technologies

654. *Anticipating the Effects of Library Systems and Networks on Space Requirements,* by Julius R. Chitwood. Paper presented at the American Library Association Annual Conference, 95th, Chicago, July 18-24, 1976. ERIC ED 129246.

> Reviews the potential impact of future changes in library technical processing activities on optimal space utilization. The article concludes that although technology may reduce current technical process space requirements, these spaces will be consumed by new services, resulting in no net gain in space availability.

655. *Automation, Space Management, and Productivity: A Guide for Libraries,* by Elaine Cohen and Aaron Cohen. New York: R.R. Bowker, 1981.

> Overview work that relates the physical planning of libraries to the people who use the facility and to productivity, with emphasis on aesthetics, function and

behavior. Topics covered include the human touch, planning, computers, space management, facility design and productivity, systems furniture, acoustics and energy conservation. Includes photographs, floor plans, checklists, diagrams, sample program requirements, ergonomic diagrams and a bibliography.

656. "Beyond Technology or Computers Are Not Enough," by A.J. Diamond. *Canadian Library Journal* 39(1982): 206-209.

Reviews the potential impacts of new technology on space allocation and layout in libraries. Includes layouts and floor plans.

657. "Building Services and Environmental Needs of Information Technology in Academic Libraries," by Dennis Heathcote and Peter Stubley. *Program* 20(1986): 26-38.

Provides guidelines for the planning and implementation of new technologies in library buildings. Includes a bibliography.

658. *College Library Buildings in Transition: Looking at the 1980's*, by Richard Snyder. Paper presented at the Conference on College and Academic Library Buildings in the 80's, New Stanton, Pennsylvania, October 14-15, 1983. ERIC, 1983. ERIC ED 2410507.

Reviews the likely impacts of new technologies on library facility design. Topics covered include problems involved in making projections, design and construction and library space requirements.

659. *Circulation, Systems, and Space: A Commentary on Interrelationships*, by Dorothy Sinclair. Paper presented at the American Library Association Annual Conference, 95th, Chicago, Illinois, July 18-24, 1976. ERIC, 1976. ERIC ED 129289.

Examines the potential impacts that membership in various networks, systems or consortia could have on space requirements in a library building.

660. "Designed for Users," by Nolan Lushington. *Wilson Library Bulletin* 57(1983): 496-498.

Describes how three Colorado public libraries (Boulder, Aurora, and Pike's Peak) have been designed to accommodate new electronic technologies. Provides description of problems and benefits associated with such an approach.

661. "Financing New Technologies, Equipment/Furniture Replacement and Building Renovation: a Survey Report," by Gary M. Shirk. *College and Research Libraries* 45(1984): 462-470.

Reports the research results of a study looking at how large public and academic libraries finance building renovations and the replacement of furniture and equipment, with special emphasis on the requirements of new technologies. Includes tables, a list of the survey participants, and a bibliography.

662. *Human Aspects of Library Automation: Helping Staff and Patrons Cope*, edited by Deborah Shaw. (Clinic on Library Applications and Processing, 1985) Urbana: Graduate School of Library and Information Science, University of Illinois, 1986.

Several of the papers in this collection deal with various technology related concerns of planning library facilities, including work station design and accommodating handicapped users. Includes bibliographies.

663. "Implementation: Preparing the Site," by Susan B. Epstein. *Library Journal* 108(1983): 2142-2143.

Reviews the site related decisions that must be reached when installing an automated library system at a site remote from the library. Factors considered include the size of the site, environmental issues, cleanliness, electrical power, security and safety, site certification, telecommunications and terminal sites.

664. "The Influence of EDP on Library Building and Management," by Paul Niewalda. *LIBER Bulletin* 25(1986): 64-66.

Part of a special issue on buildings and new technology, this article looks at the process used to plan and implement automated systems at the University of Regensburg. Includes a bibliography.

665. *Information Technologies and Space Planning for Libraries and Information Centers*, by Richard W. Boss. Boston: G.K. Hall, 1987.

While focusing for the most part on the new technologies themselves, this work also looks at their implications for space planning in libraries. Includes illustrations and a bibliography.

666. "Information Technology and Space Planning." *Library Systems Newsletter* 5(1985): 81-83.

Reviews the increasing importance of including the requirements of new technology when planning library facilities. Topics covered include ergonomics, work space, power and telecommunications requirements, and lighting.

667. "Integrating New Technology: Some Architectural Solutions," by Wesley J. Cochran. *Law Library Journal* 70(1979): 542-548.

Discusses the architectural problems being brought on

by recent technological advances and possible solutions
to these problems that can be utilized by library
facility planners.

668. "Library Automation: Building and Equipment
Considerations in Implementing Computer Technology," by
Edwin B. Brownrigg. *Advances in Library Administration and
Organization*, edited by Gerard B. McCabe, et al. 1(1982):
43-53.

Provides detailed checklists for the planning and
implementation of automation in a library facility.
Topics covered include scheduling, building requirements,
system layout, floor construction, furniture, acoustics,
electromagnetic compatibility, lighting, air conditioning,
temperature and humidity control, air filtration, power
requirements, power distribution systems, safety and fire
precautions and security analysis. Includes a brief
bibliography.

669. "Library Buildings in the Network Environment," by
Margaret Beckman. *Journal of Academic Librarianship*
9(1983): 281-284.

Looks at the likely impact of new technologies on
library facility planning and design. Topics covered
include space allocation and organization, functional
relationships of different building areas, staff space
requirements, user requirements, and mechanical, power
and structural requirements.

670. "Library Environment for Automated Systems:
Guidelines," by James A. Damico and Kenneth E. Marks.
LAMA Newsletter (1986): 28-32.

Discusses the major factors related to designing for
new technologies and makes recommendations, including
site considerations (location, storage facilities, floor,
acoustics, illumination, vibration, fire safety), air
conditioning (systems specifications, airborne

contaminants), electrical requirements (power requirements, service voltage, power distribution, grounding, installing line treatment devices, electromagnetic compatibility), facility maintenance (cleanliness, air-conditioning system maintenance, power maintenance) and detection equipment and security devices (temperature and humidity, water, smoke and ionization, power controls, warning systems). Includes a bibliography.

671. *Managing the Library Automation Project*, by John Corbin. Phoenix: Oryx Press, 1985.

Within the broad context of planning and implementing an automated system, this book contains a chapter on site preparation. Topics covered include room specifications, site selection, layout, construction, telecommunications, and work station design and equipment. Includes sample specifications and layouts.

672. "The New Technology and the Design of Library Buildings," by Jack E. Brown. *Running Out of Space: What are the Alternatives?*, edited by Gloria Novak. Proceedings of a Preconference at the American Library Association Annual Meeting, 1975. Chicago: American Library Association, 1978. 65-75.

Describes how the facility for the Canada Institute for Scientific and Technical Information was planned and designed to accommodate current and future technological developments and requirements, including user and staff needs, storage, intra-building communication, inter-building communication, reprography and computer facilities. Includes a transcription of a discussion by the preconference participants.

673. "Present and Future Trends in Library Design and Planning," by Mildred F. Schmertz. *Architectural Record* 153(1973): 119-136.

Reviews the impact of current and future trends in the planning and design of public and academic library buildings, using several new libraries as examples. Also emphasizes the particular potential impact of new communication technologies.

674. "Radiation, Ergonomics, Ion Depletion, and VDTs: Healthful Use of Visual Display Terminals," by Bruce Miller. *Information Technology and Libraries* 2(1983): 151-158.

Discusses health hazards that may be associated with the use of visual display terminals. Provides ergonomic guidelines for the design of VDT workstations, including design of work station, design of VDT, and illumination and glare. Includes an annotated bibliography.

675. "A Room of Their Own: Optional Setting for Patrons and Patron Computers" by Richard E.Thompson. *Technical Services Quarterly* 2.3/4(1985): 73-91.

Describes the planning and construction of a special room in a public library designed to house computers owned by patrons. Includes illustrations.

676. "Working Within the Systems," by Gloria Novak. *American Libraries* 19(1988): 270-271.

Advocates the use of office-landscape furniture systems in libraries as a means of efficiently and effectively using new technology equipment and systems. Includes photographs.

2.6 Signage and Guiding

677. "Butler Library Displays Vital Signs," by Carlo R. Piech. *College and Research Libraries News* 6(1986): 379-381.

Describes improved signage system at E.H. Butler
Library at Buffalo State College. Reviews the planning,
implementation and impact of the new system. Includes
illustrations.

678. *Committee on Library Orientation Report to the Directors
Council on a Library Sign System*, by Linda Lester, et al.
Charlottesville; University of Virginia, 1980. ERIC ED
196452.

Provides a rationale for a unified well-designed sign
system in the University of Virginia library. Gives
recommendations for different types of signs, interior
and exterior signs, implementation and installation of
sign systems, the use of a design consultant,
installation priorities and in-house production facilities.
Includes a bibliography and the survey instrument.

679. *Creating the Library Identity: A Manual of Design*, by
John Kirby. Brookfield: Gower Publishing, 1985.

This manual is designed to help librarians inexperienced
in graphic design and signage develop a system for
their libraries. Includes discussions, accompanied by
numerous examples, of setting up the identity program,
tools and equipment, materials and processes, formats,
layout and design, typography, guiding (signing) the
library, guiding the collection, services and procedures,
library stationery, publishing for sale and dealing with
the professional. Includes glossary, color microfiche,
non-copyrighted worksheet packet and a bibliography.

680. "Decisions, Decisions, Decisions," by John Kupersmith.
Research Strategies 1.4(1983): 182-184.

Looks at the types of decisions that must be made
when planning and implementing a successful library
sign system, including a list of questions which should
be asked and answered as part of the process. Includes
a brief bibliography.

681. *Directional Signing and Labelling in Libraries and Museums: A Review of Current Theory and Practice,* by Herbert Spencer and Linda Reynolds. London: Royal College of Art, 1977.

> Reports a study of how signage is used in 27 libraries and 17 museums, with an emphasis on directional signs and systems. Includes illustrations and a bibliography.

682. "A Good Library Sign System," by Peter R. Van Allen. *Reference Services Review* 12.2(1984): 102-106.

> Reviews common library signage problems and provides several recommendations for a quality sign system. Includes photographs.

683. "Graphic Design in Libraries," by Povl Abrahamsen. *Library Interior Layout and Design,* edited by Rolf Fuhlrott and Michael Dewe. Proceedings of the Seminar Held in Frederiksdal, Denmark, June 16-20, 1980. (IFLA Publications 24) New York: K.G. Saur, 1982. 94-105.

> Provides an overview of library signage design. Topics covered include the guiding plan, reading signs, perception, choice of lettering, harmony in the environment, sizes of signs, colors and color-coding, pictograms and the lighting of signs.

684. "A Guide to Library Environmental Graphics," by Wayne Kosterman. *Library Technology Reports* 14(1978): 269-295.

> Detailed overview of the role of signage in libraries and the effective design and use of sign systems. Topics covered include planning, content, location, and construction. Includes tables, illustrations and a bibliography.

685. "Informational Graphics and Sign Systems as Library Instruction Media," by John Kupersmith. *Drexel Library Quarterly* 16.1(1980): 54-68.

Discusses how to design an effective sign system and how such a system can be utilized in library instruction, regulation, orientation and current awareness. Includes illustrations and a bibliography.

686. *Library Guiding: A Program for Exploiting Library Resources*, by R.J.P. Carey. London: Clive Bingley, 1974.

Overview of different types of guiding systems in libraries, including signs. Includes illustrations, tables and bibliographies.

687. *Library Sign Systems. Workshop Program Materials*, by Patricia M. Ridgeway. Materials developed for the South Carolina Library Association, Public Services Section Workshop at Columbia, South Carolina on April 19, 1979. ERIC ED 176726.

These program materials include a news story on workshop, notes in outline form from a speech by a graphics designer and an annotated bibliography on signs and sign systems.

688. "New Directions in Library Signage: You Can Get There From Here," by Dorothy Pollet. *Wilson Library Bulletin* 50(1976): 456-462.

Interview with library interior designer David Pesanelli, covering the basics of library signage.

689. *Plan for a Sign System at the Idaho State University Library*, by Douglas Birdsall. Potacello: University Libraries, Idaho State University, 1980. ERIC ED 191441.

Reviews the importance of a well planned signage

system and describes such a system developed for an academic library. Includes an examination of the literature and a bibliography.

690. *A Sign System for Libraries,* by Mary S. Mallery and Ralph E. DeVore. Chicago: American Library Association, 1982.

This manual is designed to allow librarians to design a comprehensive and unified graphic sign system. Topics covered include a glossary of graphics arts terms, typography, terminology, symbols, mounting, construction, exterior sign locations, maintenance and manufacturers, publications and forms, and special signs. Includes examples, mounting drawings and construction diagrams.

691. "A Sign System for the University of Auckland Library," by Valerie Richards. *New Zealand Libraries* 44.1(1983): 12-15.

Describes the planning and implementation of a sign system in a new academic main library, in which students were used to carry out the actual design and building of the signs. Also briefly examines sign systems in other New Zealand libraries. Includes illustrations and a bibliography.

692. *Sign Systems for Libraries: Solving the Wayfinding Problem,* edited and compiled by Dorothy Pollet and Peter C. Haskell. New York: R.R. Bowker, 1979.

Collection of separately authored papers dealing with a wide variety of signage related issues, including theory and research, visual guidance systems, practical library solutions, and signage and the building. Looks at signage for the handicapped and for school, public, academic and special libraries. Appendix considers the technical and psychological aspects of library signage. Includes numerous illustrations, tables and an annotated bibliography.

693. "Signs and Graphic Displays: A Survey of Their Use in Public Libraries," by Susan Grimley. Thesis. University of Chicago, 1974.

> Reports a study of the effectiveness of the signage and graphic displays used in 39 medium sized public libraries. Includes tables and a bibliography.

694. "Signs and Guides: Wayfinding Alternatives for the EMS Library," by Johana H. Johnson. Dissertation. University of California at Los Angeles, 1981.

> Gives the results of a study at the Engineering and Math Sciences Library at UCLA, presenting an overview of library sign systems and contrasting them with other types of self-guidance systems. Includes a discussion of such factors as signage hierarchy, communication, typography and layout. Also includes the survey questionnaire, the pretest results, the raw data, a library guide evaluation sheet, photographs, tables and a bibliography.

695. *Signs and Guiding for Libraries*, by Linda Reynolds and Stephen Barrett. London: Clive Bingley, 1981.

> This detailed coverage of library signage includes consideration of sign location and content, principles of sign design, materials and methods, design principles in practice, sign production, publications and stationery, and project management. Includes a list of manufacturers and suppliers, and a bibliography.

2.7 Moving

696. "Collection Shifting---From Crowding to User Comfort," by Martha L. Faller. *The New Library Scene* 3(1984): 9-10, 17.

Describes the process used by the Niagara County
Community College library to shift the collection from a
crowded condition to a more evenly-spaced one. Includes
instructions for counting the shelves, estimating the
number of full shelves, analyzing collection growth and
two plans for shifting. Also includes tables.

697. "A Committee Approach to Moving a Library: Planning,
Personnel and Stress," by Pat Weaver-Meyers and Dale F.
Wasowski. *Journal of Library Administration* 5.4(1984): 21-32.

Describes the process used to plan and implement the
move of the 900,000 volume Bizzell Library at the
University of Oklahoma, with an emphasis on the
personnel concerns involved in such an operation.

698. "Creating a New Facility for Ayerst Laboratories
Research, Inc." by Barbara Boyajian. *Science and Technology
Libraries* 7.1(1986): 3-14.

Part of a special issue on library buildings, this article
describes the planning and implementing of the move of
a pharmaceutical library. Also describes the new
facility, including basic statistics, a photograph and a
layout drawing.

699. "Creating New Library Facilities for the Bendix
Advanced Technology Center," by Ted Rupprecht. *Science and
Technology Libraries* 3.4(1983): 59-75.

Reports on the move of a scientific special library in
Michigan to a new facility in Maryland. Includes
illustrations, table and a brief bibliography.

700. "The Development of a Computer-Based Library System:
LCDF - Library Collection Distribution Formulas," by Donna
L. Kurkul. MLS Thesis. State University of New York at
Albany, 1982. ERIC ED 234777.

Reports development and testing of a software package
designed to permit calculation of optimum collection
distribution and sequences prior to a physical move.
Includes draft version of a user manual, sample run of
the program, sample results, tables, and a bibliography.

701. *From Here to There: Moving a Library*, by Dennis C.
Tucker. Bristol: Wyndham Hall, 1987.

Detailed examination of the moving process, including
both planning and implementation aspects. Includes
illustrations and a bibliography.

702. "Helpful Hints for Moving or Shifting Collections," by
Anthony J. Amodeo. *College and Research Library News*
44.3(1983): 82-83

Provides practical guidelines for organizing and carrying
out a collection shift or move. Includes drawing
showing how to load and organize a bookcart.

703. "How to Move a Library in One Easy Lesson," by
Mark Ames. *Michigan Librarian* 39(1973): 30-31.

Describes moving a public library to temporary housing
in a former train depot.

704. "Library Moving Procedure," by Jane A. Schuyler.
Planning the Special Library, edited by Ellis Mount. (SLA
Monograph no. 4) New York: Special Libraries Association,
1972. 52-54.

Presents recommendations for planning and implementing
the move of special libraries. Topics covered include
preliminary planning, equipment and aids.

705. "Library Removal: It Could Happen to You," by Helen
Stoddart and Lesley Hughes. *New Zealand Libraries*

44.5(1984): 83-84.

Describes the planning and implementation of the move of the Ministry of Agriculture and Fisheries Central Library in New Zealand to a space smaller than the original location.

706. "Moving a Large Library," by Robert F. Moran, Jr. *Special Libraries* 63(1972): 163-171.

Reports the move of the University of Chicago Library of 1,800,000 volumes from 11 buildings to the Joseph Regenstein Library and the integration of 1,580,000 of these volumes into one collection. Includes a discussion of the book move plan, book distribution within the stacks of the new facility, methods used to move the books, furniture and equipment required for the move, problems related to moving into an unfinished facility and evaluation. Includes photographs and tables.

707. "Moving a Medical Center Library," by Britain G. Roth. *Special Libraries* 76(1985): 31-34.

Describes the process used to move a 30,000 book and journal collection and 600 nonprint items at the Geisinger Medical Center library. Topics covered include space planning, service disruptions, staff morale and physical handling. Includes a bibliography.

708. "Moving a Public Library Collection," by Patricia Hamilton and Pam Hindman. *Public Libraries* 26(1987): 4-7.

Looks at the planning and implementation of the move of the Cedar Rapids Public Library. Examines the importance of good communication, the use of teams, computer support, volunteers and the move itself. Includes illustrations.

709. "Moving an Academic Library," by Sam E. Ifidon.

Journal of Academic Librarianship 4(1979): 434-437.

Describes the move of a 150,000 volume collection to a new building.

710. "Moving an Academic Library: A Case Study," by A.E. Lumb. *Journal of Librarianship* 4(1972): 253-271.

Reviews important factors to be considered when moving an academic library, including timing, consideration of different methods, selection of a mover, preparation, preliminary work and the move itself. Includes detailed lists of specific points and a bibliography.

711. "Moving Steel Stacks with a Special Dolly," by Brian Alley. *Library Acquisition: Practice and Theory* 6(1982): 253-257.

Describes a dolly designed to allow the easy movement of stack ranges using a minimum of person-power. Includes drawings and instructions on how to construct the dolly.

712. "New Map Room Opens at the University of Nevada, Reno," by Mary B. Ansari. *Bulletin of the Geography and Map Division (SLA)* 116(1979): 40-42.

Reports the move of the School of Mines Library into new space in the University's main library. Particular problems encountered included having to split the collection up for storage in several small rooms. Includes a floor plan.

713. "The Planning, Implementation and Movement of an Academic Library Collection," by Donna Lee Kurkul. *College and Research Libraries* 44(1983): 220-234.

Following a brief literature review, this article discusses

how the Neilson Library at Smith College moved its 682,810 volume collection throughout a major construction and renovation project. Provides details on the process, including methodology, formulas for determining collection sequence distributions, formulas for determining number of shelves required, estimation of person-power and time requirements and the ramifications of using temporary employees. Includes tables, a brief bibliography and two appendices dealing with the calculation of formulas.

714. "Pulling the Rug Out From Under the Stacks," by James Segesta. *College and Research Libraries News* 47(1986): 441-444.

Describes how Cumberland County College in New Jersey moved fully loaded, double-faced ranges that were six sections long.

715. "Remodeled Library Facilities for the Ontario Regional Primate Research Center," by Isabel G. McDonald. *Science and Technology Libraries* 3.4(1983): 21-30.

Describes the move of a small biomedical library to a renovated larger facility. Includes illustrations and a brief bibliography.

716. "Reorganizing a School Library Resource Center," by Janet Stevenson. *School Librarian* 27(1979): 108-111.

Reports on the organization and move of the Stoke High School in Ipswich, England into a new library facility, giving details on materials organization and the use of parents as volunteers.

3.0 ENVIRONMENTAL, MECHANICAL, ELECTRICAL AND SECURITY SYSTEMS

3.1 Environmental Design: Preservation, Disasters and Maintenance

717. "After the Disaster: Restoring Library Service," by Jack W. Griffith. *Wilson Library Bulletin* 58(1983): 258-265.

Reviews various types of library related disasters and presents recommendations on various equipment and facility design factors that can reduce the chance of a problem. Topics covered include alarm systems, secure doors, lighting, landscaping, book returns, sightlines, mirrors, plastic furniture, electric power systems and fire detection systems. Also discusses how to deal with a disaster after it has taken place.

718. "Air Conditioning Design for a Fixed Humidity Environment," *Heating, Piping, Air Conditioning* 55(1983): 57-61.

Describes the environmental control system at the Library for the Health Sciences at the University of Kansas Medical Center. The special collections require a temperature of 75 degrees and a fixed 50 percent relative humidity. The article includes charts showing humidification costs, chiller configurations, a chilled water piping schematic and a condensed water piping schematic.

719. "Air Conditioning for Archives," by Timothy Walsh. *Archives and Manuscripts* 8.2(1980): 70-78.

Provides guidelines for air conditioning systems for archival facilities. Includes illustrations and a bibliography.

720. "Beset by Foes on Every Side," by Pamela W. Darling. *Disasters: Prevention and Coping,* edited by James N. Myers and Denise D. Bedford. Proceedings of the Conference, May 21-22, 1980. Stanford: Stanford University Libraries, 1981. 18-23.

Discusses environmental control aspects of disaster prevention, including light, temperature, humidity, mold, insects, airborne contaminants and ventilation.

721. "Conservation and Preservation of Archives," by Y.P. Kathpalia. *Unesco Journal of Information Science, Librarianship and Archives Administration* 4.2(1982): 94-100.

Describes preventive conservation techniques for archival facilities, including environmental control, storage approaches, and fire prevention. Includes a brief bibliography.

722. *Conservation in the Library: A Handbook of Use and Care of Traditional and Nontraditional Materials,* edited by Susan G. Swartzburg. Westport: Greenwood Press, 1983.

This book is divided into chapters by types of materials, including paper books and bindings, photographs, slides, microforms, motion-picture film, videotape, sound recordings, and video discs. Environmental control requirements for each material type is covered. A chapter on general care reviews the roles of light, temperature and humidity, light, mold and fungi and pests. Includes photographs, drawings, tables, and bibliographies.

723. "Conservation of Library Material in Tropical Conditions: The Example of Nigeria," by O.O. Ogundipe. Paper presented at the Annual Conference of the International Federation of Library Associations, Manila, Philippines, August 18-23, 1980. ERIC, 1980. ERIC ED 211037.

Examines the special problems associated with conserving materials in a high heat and high humidity climate. Current Nigerian facilities and their problems are discussed. Includes a bibliography.

724. "Conservation of Library Materials and the Environment: A Study with Recommendations," by Elizabeth A. Teo. *Illinois Libraries* 67 (1985): 711-717.

Reviews the role of environmental control in library conservation, including a report on a temperature and humidity study done at Moraine Valley Community College library. Includes recommendations for environmental control and a bibliography.

725. "Conservation of Photographs: Some Thoughts and References," *Art Libraries Journal* 5(1980): 5-11.

Reviews British standards on photograph conservation, including a discussion of storage, atmospheric pollution and damp, mold, heat, and light. Includes a bibliography.

726. *A Conservation Plan for the Transylvania University Library*, by Kathleen Bryson and Lynn Mayo. ERIC, 1981. ERIC ED 214495.

A self-study of the conservation needs of the Frances Corrick Thomas Library, including a consideration of the architectural and environmental problems of the existing building. Provides short-term, intermediate and long-term recommendations. Includes a bibliography.

727. *Determination of the Environmental Conditions Required in a Library for the Effective Utilization of Microforms: Interim Report*, by Donald C. Holmes. Washington, DC: Association of Research Libraries, 1970. ERIC ED 046403.

Presents environmental control guidelines for microforms, including coverage of both user and materials needs.

728. *Disaster Manual: Emergency, Evacuation, Recovery*, by Brad Koplowitz, et al. Oklahoma City: Oklahoma State Department of Libraries, 1982. ERIC ED 215676.

This manual outlines the responsibilities of library staff at the Oklahoma State Library in the event of an emergency situation. Includes library floor plans showing exit routes and emergency operation procedures. Also includes a safety checklist, information about fire extinguishers and materials recovery procedures.

729. *Disaster Preparedness: A Guide for Developing a Plan to Cope with Disaster for the Public and Private Library* Durham: Duke University Library, 1982.

Guide for dealing with disaster situations, largely those related to floods and other types of water damage. Briefly discusses the role of environmental control in terms of temperature, humidity and mold. Includes list of conservators and a bibliography.

730. *Disaster Preparedness Manual*, by Douglas O. Michael. Auburn: Cayaga County Community College, 1981. ERIC ED 208887.

Reviews natural, human, and building hazards which can potentially result in disaster in the Bourke Memorial Library. The building hazards identified include water pipes and plumbing, roof drainage and roof leaks, basement drainage, electrical system, mechanical rooms, elevator and chair lift. Recommendations are provided for prevention of floods.

Floor plans are given, as is a procedure for evacuation of the elevator.

731. *Disasters: Prevention and Coping*, edited by James N. Myers and Denise D. Bedford. Proceedings of the Conference, May 21-22, 1980. Stanford: Stanford University Libraries, 1981.

Within the broad context of disaster prevention, these proceedings include several papers related to facilities design. These papers, which are treated individually in this bibliography are "Fire," by John Morris, "Beset by foes on every side," by Pamela W. Darling, "The quiet disaster II: pests and people," by Gay Walker and "Reducing preservation hazards within library facilities," by Philip D. Leighton.

732. "Effects of Temperature and Humidity on Film," by E.A. Collister. *APLA Bulletin* 42.5(1979): 4-5.

Looks at the environmental control and design requirements for film-based audiovisual materials. Provides specific temperature and humidity guidelines. Includes a bibliography.

733. *Emergencies and Problems: A Procedures Manual for Trinity University Library*, by Katherine D. Pettit. San Antonio: Trinity University, 1981. ERIC ED 214527.

This manual is divided into six sections dealing with various types of emergencies. Building related problems covered include elevator failure, fire, flooding and power failure. Floor plans showing fire alarms, fire extinguishers and fire stairs are appended.

734. *Environmental Control for Regional Library Facilities*, by Richard G. King. (RR-80-3) Berkeley: University of California Systemwide Administration, 1980. ERIC ED 2002222.

An overview of the problems caused by environmental factors, including atmospheric pollutants, temperature control and humidity control.

735. "Environmental Factors Affecting the Permanence of Library Materials," by Carl J. Wessel. *Library Quarterly* 40(1970): 39-84.

An in-depth review of the environmental factors relevant to library materials preservation. Considers such aspects as atmospheric pollution, light, temperature, humidity, vibration, parasites and molds, people, disasters and mechanical system failures. Includes tables and an extensive bibliography.

736. "Environmental Standards for Storage of Books and Manuscripts," by Paul N. Banks. *Library Journal* 99(1974): 339-343.

Discusses the environmental control aspects of facility design, including temperature, humidity, air cleanliness, ventilation, light, exhibitions, shelving and transportation, storage of microfilm, disaster control and monitoring systems. Includes illustrations and a bibliography.

737. "Fire," by John Morris. *Disasters: Prevention and Coping*, edited by James N. Myers and Denise D. Bedford. Proceedings of the Conference May 21-22, 1980. Stanford: Stanford University Libraries, 1981. 13-17.

Reviews the causes of recent library fires, followed by a discussion of the standard defenses some libraries use to reduce the chance of fire and to make control easier should a fire get started.

738. *Guidelines for Preventive Conservation*, by Joyce M. Banks. Ottawa, Canada: Council of Federal Libraries, 1981.

Explains the role that planned preventive strategies can

play in the conservation of library materials, including environmental factors and appropriate storage configurations. Includes a bibliography.

739. "Health Science Library Materials: Preservation," by Stanley D. Truelson, Jr. *Handbook of Medical Library Practice*, edited by Louise Darling. 4th edition. Vol. 2. Chicago: Medical Library Association, 1983. 139-182.

Facility design preservation concerns are covered in an "environmental protection" section of this chapter. Issues addressed include light, heat, humidity, mildew and mold, air pollution, pests, chemicals, fire and water. Includes an extensive bibliography.

740. "The Ideal Preservation Building," by Bonnie Jo Cullison. *American Libraries* 15(1984): 703.

Describes the bookstack building of the Newberry Library and how it was designed and is operated for preservation purposes, including a discussion of the environmental control standards used by the library.

741. *Iowa Statewide Disaster Recovery Plan*, edited by Barry L. Porter. Des Moines: Iowa State Library Commission, 1981. ERIC ED 217834.

Plan developed as an aid for local libraries designing their own disaster preparedness plans. Includes fire and insurance coverage questionnaire which includes the library building. Also includes several other self-assessment forms and a bibliography.

742. *The Library Disaster Preparedness Handbook*, by John Morris. Chicago: American Library Association, 1986.

Overview of various disaster situations for libraries. Facilities related issues covered include basic building security, fire-safe design and construction, automatic fire

suppression and detection systems, planning and design
for safety and security, glass, stairs, lights, entrances
and exits, interior design, elevators, doors and windows,
site, fire and water, temperature and humidity, air
quality, lighting and conservation, pests and insurance.
Includes illustrations, photographs, tables, glossary and
a bibliography.

743. "Map Preservation: An Overview," by Arlyn Sherwood.
Illinois Libraries 67(1985): 705-711.

Reviews the handling and preservation of maps,
including a discussion of environmental control, shelving
and storage. Includes a bibliography.

744. "Nonprint Materials: A Definition and Some Practical
Considerations on Their Maintenance," by Thomas B. Wall.
Library Trends 34(1985): 129-140.

Beyond a basic general discussion of nonprint materials,
this article looks at such environmental issues as dust,
temperature, and light. Also covers security and storage
concerns. Includes tables and a bibliography.

745. "An Opinion on the Nitrate Film Fire, Suitland,
Maryland, 7 December 1978," by W.H Utterback, Jr.
Journal of the University Film Association 32(1980): 3-16.

Discusses storage conditions and other circumstances
which resulted in a major film storage facility fire.
Includes recommendations for preventing such disasters
in the future.

746. "Photographs: Their Care and Conservation," by
Barbara Zucker. *Illinois Libraries* 67(1985): 699-704.

Reviews the proper care of photographs, including a
section on storage, handling, and environmental control.
Includes a bibliography.

747. "A Psocid by Any Other Name---(Is Still a Pest)," by Frances R. Weinstein. *Library and Archival Security* 6(1984): 57-63.

Discusses five types of common crawling insects which often infest libraries, together with preventive measures including environmental control.

748. *Preservation and Conservation of Library Documents: A UNESCO/IFLA/ICA Enquiry into the Current State of the World's Patrimony*, edited by D.W.G. Clements. Paris: UNESCO General Information Programme and UNISIST, 1987.

Based on a 1986 survey, this report takes a detailed look at worldwide conservation and preservation concerns and strategies, including facilities related environment control. Includes the survey instrument.

749. *Preservation at Stony Brook: Preservation Planning Program, Study Report*, by Donald C. Cook, et al. Washington: Association of Research Libraries, 1985. ERIC ED 267809.

Preservation based self-study using the Preservation Planning Program developed by Association of Research Libraries. Includes sections on the physical facility, environmental conditions, and disaster control, providing an evaluation of the existing situation. Recommendations on improvements in the areas of air quality, light, flood control, fire control, security and safety standardization and guidelines, physical storage, housekeeping, food and drink and book returns are included.

750. *The Preservation Challenge: A Guide to Conserving Library Materials*, by Carolyn Clark Morrow. White Plains: Knowledge Industry, 1983.

Overview of materials preservation programs in

libraries. Discusses environmental agents of destruction, including light, heat, humidity, gaseous air pollutants, particulate matter, fungi and insects. Includes case studies of seven preservation programs, providing limited information on the preservation facilities at each program. Includes a bibliography.

751. *Preservation Conditions, Practices, and Needs in the General Libraries: A Report by the Preservation Committee.* Austin: University of Texas at Austin, 1981. ERIC ED 214503.

Presents the results of survey conducted to investigate preservation concerns in the General Libraries of the University of Texas at Austin. Includes sections on how special types of materials are handled (print, audiovisual, microforms, maps, archives, etc.) and environmental conditions (air conditioning, humidity, lighting, particulate control, etc.). Copies of the survey instruments are included, together with a discussion of recommendations based on the study. Similar studies of other academic libraries can be accessed through ERIC.

752. *Preservation of the Biomedical Literature: A Plan for the National Library of Medicine,* by Betsy L. Humphreys, et al. Washington: Association of Research Libraries, 1985. ERIC ED 265879.

Reviews preservation programs at the National Library of Medicine, which are based on the "Preservation Planning Program: An Assisted Self-Study Manual for Libraries," developed by the Association of Research Libraries. A chapter on physical facilities and environment reviews the roles temperature and relative humidity, atmospheric pollutants, light, mold, and insects and rodents play in the longevity of paper. The NLM facility is described, including reading and study areas, special collections stack areas and storage areas. Includes an appendix on specific indoor pollution conditions and methodology for their determination, at NLM. Has tables and a brief bibliography.

753. *Preservation Planning Program Resource Notebook,* compiled by Pamela W. Darling, revised edition by Wesley L. Boomgaarden. Washington: Association of Research Libraries, 1987.

> Provides very detailed bibliography on materials preservation, together with the full text of over 100 previously published articles. This work is a companion to *Preservation Planning Program: An Assisted Self-Study Manual for Libraries,* prepared by Pamela W. Darling with Duane E. Webster.

754. *Principles for the Preservation and Conservation of Library Materials,* by J.M. Dureau. (IFLA Professional Report no. 8) The Hague: International Federation of Library Associations and Institutions, 1986. ERIC ED 267823.

> A general overview of library materials preservation, including consideration of temperature, humidity, air pollution, dust and cleanliness, book delivery systems, building design, standards, fire, flood, war and natural disaster, theft, user accommodations, duplication, exhibits, lighting, pests, mold and mildew, and photograph preservation.

755. "Protecting the Library Against Fire: Some Considerations Affecting Interior Layout and Design," by Harry Faulkner-Brown. *Library Interior Layout and Design,* edited by Rolf Fuhlrott and Michael Dewe. Proceedings of the Seminar Held in Frederiksdal, Denmark, June 16-20, 1980. (IFLA Publications 24) New York: K.G. Saur, 1982. 57-69.

> Provides an overview of building design elements which can help protect the library and the library patron from fire, using the University of Newcastle Library as a case study. Includes floor plans, a site plan, section drawing, and a photograph.

756. "Protecting the Library From Fire," by John Morris.

Library Trends 33(1984): 49-56.

Reviews the actions libraries can take to reduce the potential for fire damage. Among the facility related recommendations are the use of reinforced doors and windows, automatic detection systems, sprinkler systems and fire extinguisher systems. Discusses the rationale for installing automatic sprinkler systems in bookstacks. Includes a bibliography.

757. "Quake, Rattle, and Roll: Or the Day the Coalinga Library Stood Still and Everything Else Moved," by Adele L. Watson. *Library and Archival Security* 6(1984): 1-5.

Describes the results of a major earthquake on a library designed and constructed to withstand earthquakes. Gives recommendations for preparing for this type of disaster and what to do when it happens.

758. "The Quiet Disaster II: Pests and People," by Gay Walker. *Disasters: Prevention and Coping,* edited by James N. Myers and Denise D. Bedford. Proceedings of the Conference, May 21-22, 1980. Stanford: Stanford University Libraries, 1981. 24-31.

Discusses the control of insects and problem patrons in library facilities, using the Beinecke Library at Yale as an example.

759. "Reducing Preservation Hazards Within Library Facilities," by Philip D. Leighton. *Disasters: Prevention and Coping,* edited by James N. Myers and Denise D. Bedford. Proceedings of the Conference, May 21-22, 1980. Stanford: Stanford University Libraries, 1981. 32-40.

Discusses facility design factors related to preservation in libraries. Topics covered include the roof, drains, walls, floor loading and leaks.

760. *Selective Bibliography on the Conservation of Research Library Materials,* by Paul N. Banks. Chicago: Newberry Library, 1981.

> Detailed non-annotated conservation bibliography. Facility related topics include conservation facilities, environmental enemies of paper, disaster, environmental control, handling and shelving, storage of nonbook materials (maps, photographs, microforms, sound recordings), exhibition, maintenance, library and archives buildings, and security.

761. "The Stanford Flood," by Philip D. Leighton. *College and Research Libraries* 40(1979): 450-459.

> Describes a major flood at the Stanford University Libraries. Includes facility design recommendations for both preventing a flood and dealing with one that has already occurred. Includes photographs and a bibliography.

762. "The Yale Survey: A Large Scale Study of Book Deterioration in the Yale University Library," by Gay Walker, et al. *College and Research Libraries* 46(1985): 111-132.

> Reports the results of a major survey of the physical conditions of books in the Yale University Library system. Includes evaluation of environmental conditions related to temperature and humidity. Also includes a bibliography and appendices giving sampling methodology and the survey instructions.

3.2 Lighting

763. *CIBS Lighting Guide: Libraries.* London: Chartered Institution of Building Services, 1982.

Provides lighting guidelines for library facilities. Includes tables, illustrations and a bibliography.

764. "Designed for Users," by Nolan Lushington. *Wilson Library Bulletin* 55(1981): 606-607, 637-638.

Describes the role of lighting in successful library design. Topics covered include how people use light, natural and indirect light, artificial light and lighting systems.

765. *Library Lighting*, by Keyes D. Metcalf. Washington: Association of Research Libraries, 1970.

Detailed consideration of lighting in libraries. Discusses lighting problems, followed by answers to lighting questions and comments by architects, engineers, consultants, interior designers, medical experts, financial officers, maintenance and physical plant officers, and research scholars. Presents conclusions and both general and specific recommendations. Includes tables and a bibliography.

766. "Lighting a New College Library: A Question of Function and Esthetics." *Lighting Design and Application* 2(1972): 14-17.

Examines basic problems faced when designing lighting systems for libraries, including flexible operation for round the clock use, installations complementary to the structural design and the required architectural innovations, sufficient illumination for critical visual tasks, and the ability to create variety while unifying the space to enhance the environment.

767. "Lighting and Air Conditioning in Libraries," by Lester K. Smith. *Planning Library Buildings: From Decision to Design*, edited by Lester K. Smith. Papers from a Preconference at the 1984 American Library Association

Annual Conference, Dallas, Texas. Chicago: Library
Administration and Management Association, American
Library Association, 1986. 163-174.

This paper is a general review of the important
aspects of both topics. Lighting topics covered include
general considerations, types of lighting, and quantity
and quality of lighting. Air conditioning topics considered
include building design, heating and cooling, humidity,
filtration, air circulation and special concerns.

768. "Lighting Design: A Missed Opportunity." *American
School and University* (1978): 40-42.

Reports a study at the graduate library of the
University of Connecticut that resulted in substantial
energy savings because of a new lighting design.

769. "On Library Lighting," by Rolf Fuhlrott. *Library Interior
Layout and Design*, edited by Rolf Fuhlrott and Michael
Dewe. Proceedings of the Seminar Held in Frederiksdal,
Denmark, June 16-20, 1980. (IFLA Publications 24) New
York: K.G. Saur, 1982. 106-118.

Reviews the role of both natural and artificial light in
libraries. The advantages and disadvantages of natural
light are covered. Aspects of artificial lighting included
are visual tasks, lighting problems, quality, intensity,
cost and methods of artificial lighting in different
library areas (reading, stack). Includes photographs.

770. "On the Verge of a Revolution: Current Trends in
Library Lighting," by Bradley A. Waters and Willis C.
Winters. *Library Trends* 36(1987): 327-349.

Part of a special issue on library buildings, this article
reports recent and continuing trends in library lighting.
Topics covered include intensity, contrast, glare,
daylight, incandescent, fluorescent, high-intensity
discharge, metal halide, pressurized sodium, mercury

vapor, and direct and indirect. Also looks at the use of daylight as a resource and light requirements for specific functional areas including stacks and storage, work areas, microfilm readers and computer terminals, carrels, reading areas, circulation, exhibits, storage areas, and emergency lighting. Includes a table, several drawings and a bibliography.

771. "Some Aspects of Library Illumination," by Rajwant Singh. *Herald of Library Science* 1(1978): 31-48.

Overview of lighting problems and their possible solutions in library environments. Recommends the use of a lighting team. Includes a table and a bibliography.

3.3 Mechanical and Electrical Systems

772. "The Asbestos Hazard in Libraries," by Robert F. Nardini. *Library Journal* 109(1984): 2001-2004.

Reviews the problems that the presence of asbestos in library facilities can cause, including basic information about asbestos and possible strategies that can be followed once it is identified. Includes illustrations and a bibliography.

773. "Asbestos is Bad News," by Lester Stoffel and Ronald S. Kozlowski. *Illinois Libraries* 67(1985): 816-818.

Reviews problems associated with asbestos in libraries built before 1974. Discusses how asbestos can be removed and the impact this has on the functioning of the facility.

774. "But Where Do I Plug the Carrel In?" by Gaylen B. Kelley. *School Media Quarterly* 2(1974): 260-267. Reprinted in *Media Center Facilities Design,* compiled and edited by Jane

A. Hannigan and Glenn E. Estes. Chicago: American Library Association, 1978. 66-71.

Discusses planning designing a media centers' electrical power systems. Includes illustrations and a bibliography.

775. "Designed for Users," by Nolan Lushington. *Wilson Library Bulletin* 56(1982): 362-363.

Discusses the factor of temperature control in designing a library. Provides overview on use of passive solar energy and air conditioning, together with basic questions to ask when making decisions about heating, ventilation and air conditioning (HVAC) systems.

776. "Mechanical Systems and Libraries," by Fred Dubin. *Library Trends* 36(1987): 351-360.

Part of a special issue on buildings, this article looks at basic mechanical system factors that should be considered when planning a library facility. Topics covered include the role and responsibilities of the planning team, raised floors, lighting, air quality, acoustics and climate controls.

777. "Physical Conditions and Their Influence on Library Layout and Design," by J. Boot. *Library Interior Layout and Design,* Edited by Rolf Fuhlrott and Michael Dewe. Proceedings of the Seminar held in Frederiksdal, Denmark, June 16-20, 1980. (IFLA Publications 24) New York: K.G. Saur, 1982. 838-93.

Discusses how the interior climates of a library building are impacted by physical conditions. Among the factors included are air temperature, radiation temperature, humidity, air circulation, cleaning the air and sound. Uses the Rotterdam Central Library to illustrate how the interior climate factors function. Includes a floor plan and photographs.

3.4 Energy Conservation and Non-Traditional Energy Systems

778. *Energy and the Cultural Community. A Report to the National Endowment for the Arts,* by Robert A. Matthai. Sponsored by the EXXON Corporation. New York: National Endowment for the Arts, 1979. ERIC ED 185670.

> Reports the results of a study which assesses the energy needs of the US cultural community, including archives and libraries. Presents findings and recommendations on six basic energy related issues, including energy efficient architecture and design.

779. "Energy Conservation and Library Design," by William C. Tippens. *Library Space Planning: Issues and Approaches,* (*LJ* Special Report no. 1, edited by Karl Nyren) New York: R.R. Bowker, 1976. 63-64.

> This paper is an overview of how energy conservation can be applied in library facility design.

780. "Energy Conservation in Libraries," by Cary G. Bullock. *Library Technology Reports* 14(1978): 305-437.

> Presents a detailed overview of topic, including factors affecting energy consumption, establishing a conservation program, lighting, HVAC, the building shell, opportunities for savings, advanced technologies, financing an energy conservation program, the future and sources of assistance. Includes charts, tables, formulas, drawings, and an annotated bibliography.

781. "Energy Conservation in Library Buildings," *LIBER Bulletin* 16(1981): 46-48. Proceedings of a Seminar held in Heidelberg in November, 1980 on library architecture.

> Part of a special proceedings issue on library architecture, this article provides a 25 item discussion

list of suggestions for conserving energy in library building design.

782. "Energy Savings in the Planning of Library Buildings," by Franz Kroller. *Library Interior Layout and Design*, edited by Rolf Fuhlrott and Michael Dewe. Proceedings of the Seminar Held in Frederiksdal, Denmark, June 16-20, 1980. (IFLA Publication 24) New York: K.G. Saur, 1982. 70-82.

Reviews the advantages of energy-saving approaches in library building design. Discusses the factors of architecture, thermal comfort, climate, heat losses from buildings, waste heat recovery and prospects for the future.

783. "An Experiment in Solar Design at San Jose State University," by Jeff Paul. *College and Research Libraries News* 43(1982): 379-380.

Describes a major library that is totally dependent on solar heating and cooling for internal climate control. Explains how the system was planned and operates.

784. "Joining Nature and Technology to Save Energy: Libraries Catch the Sun," by S.E. Brandehoff. *American Libraries* 12(1981): 562-563.

Describes how three libraries use solar energy, including both conservation and aesthetic factors. Includes illustrations.

785. "Lake Villa Public Library District and Passive Solar Energy." *Illinois Libraries* 67(1985): 810-812.

Reviews the benefits associated with passive solar energy. Includes a list of minimum design components required for a successful solar design and photographs.

786. "Remodeling to Save Energy: Is it Always Cost-Effective for a Public Library," by J. Parke Randall. *Indiana Libraries* 3(1983): 100-105.

Discusses the potential positive and negative cost aspects of remodeling in terms of energy conservation. Covers problems associated with remodeling Carnegie-era libraries, in contrast to buildings built between 1940 and 1975.

787. "Solar Oriented System," by Marcia Wallach and Frank Coleman. *Library Journal* 108(1983): 2205-2208.

Reviews the construction of six public libraries and the renovation of a trucking terminal as a library, all in Mercer County, New Jersey. The buildings are designed to be energy efficient using solar energy systems. Includes photographs and floor plans.

788. "Solar Power in the Public Library," compiled by Kenneth Shearer. *Public Libraries* 20(1981): 35-36.

Includes three brief reports on the use of solar power in public libraries. Describes the solar system at the Wicomico County (MD) Free Library, and the estimated 75 percent cost savings achieved by the City of Mount Airy (NC) Library. Includes glazing diagrams for Mount Airy.

3.5 Designing for Security and Safety

789. "Architects, Security Consultants, and Security Planning for New Libraries," by John W. Powell. *Library Security Newsletter* 1(1975): 1,6-7.

Emphasizes the need to include security in the overall initial planning of a new library building. Recommends the use of professional security consultants and provides criteria for selection of a consultant.

790. "Collection Security," by Richard W. Boss. *Library Trends* 33.1(1984): 39-48.

Reviews collection related security problems including facility weaknesses. Includes an outline for a security audit.

791. *Crime in the Library: A Study of Patterns, Impact, and Security*, by Alan J. Lincoln. New York: R.R. Bowker, 1984.

This book is an overview of crime in the library. Facility related topics include perimeter security, protection of entry points, protecting interior locations, multiple point protection and visibility enhancement. Includes a detailed security checklist.

792. "Deviant Behavior in the Library," by Dale Welch. *The User Encounters the Library: An Interdisciplinary Focus on the User/System Interface*, edited by Martin B. Steffenson and Larry D. Larason. Proceedings of a Library Training Institute, Monroe, Louisiana, July 31-August 3, 1978. Monroe: Northwest Louisiana University, 1986. 1-3. ERIC ED 266791.

This paper provides an overview and definition of deviant behavior in libraries. Reviews the roles of architectural design and environmental spaces in contributing to and/or controlling such behavior, particularly theft and vandalism. Includes suggestions on restroom design, lock and key control, noise control, entrance/exit security and signs. Includes bibliography.

793. "Improving Security and Safety for Libraries," by Lee B. Brawner and Norman Nelson. *Public Library Quarterly* 5(1984): 41-57.

Discusses the planning and design of libraries from a

security and safety perspective. Details external considerations and "fortifying" the library building, including topics such as landscaping, entrance/exit control, lighting, doors, locks and keys, burglar-resistant windows, fire escapes, alarm systems and closed circuit television. Includes bibliography.

794. "Preventing Public Sex in Library Settings," Edward W. Delph. *Library and Archival Security* 3.2(1980): 17-26.

Provides facility design suggestions for controlling unwanted patron behavior in the library.

795. "Proceedings of the American Library Association Conference Program on Collection Security and Life Safety, San Francisco, June 30, 1981," by John Vasi. *Library and Archival Security* 4(1982): 9-38.

Includes three speeches on equipment and operational considerations of library security and life safety, the role and function of architectural codes in buildings and the effect of safety and security equipment on insurance rates. Includes transcriptions of question and answer sessions and an appendix on code requirements.

796. "Profiteers Among the Stacks," by Ronald G. Leach. *Library Issues: Briefings for Faculty and Administrators* 2.6(1982): 2-4.

Briefly considers the problems associated with theft of library materials and the question of closed vs. open stacks.

797. "Security of Academic Library Buildings," by Marvine Brand. *Library and Archival Security* 3(1980): 39-47.

Reviews security recommendations made for the University of Houston Library. Topics covered include perimeter, outside architectural design and landscaping, exterior barriers, public access areas and general work areas. Includes a bibliography.

798. "Security Problems in College and University Libraries: Student Violence," by Donna G. Davis. *College and Research Libraries* 32(1971): 15-22.

Overview of the impact of student violence on academic libraries, including facility design recommendations to lessen the problem.

799. "Three Studies of Library Crime," by Alan Jay Lincoln and Carol Zall Lincoln. *Library and Archival Security* 8(1986): 89-114.

Compares patterns of library crime in the United States with the patterns found in Canada and the United Kingdom, including a discussion of the role facility design plays in crime. Includes tables and a bibliography.

800. "Waging War Against Crimes in Florida's Public Libraries," by Betty A. Scott. *Library and Archival Security* 3(1980): 27-30.

Reviews various tatics that can be used to reduce crime in public libraries, including those related to facility design.

AUTHOR INDEX

SUBJECT INDEX